The Penguin Nature Library

General Editor: Edward Hoagland

SONGS OF THE NORTH

Sigurd Olson was quite possibly the most famous woodsman of our day. For more than thirty years he was a
wilderness guide in the Quetico-Superior country, and no
one knew with the same intimacy the mysteries of the
lakes and forests of that magnificent area. For several years
he taught biology at Ely Junior College (Minnesota),
where he later served as dean, and he was recognized
nationally with many awards and honorary degrees. He
served as consultant to the federal government on wilderness preservation and ecological problems, as advisor to
the Izaak Walton League of America, and as president of
the Wilderness Society and the National Parks Association.
Until his death in 1982, he made his home in Ely, gateway
to his beloved Quetico-Superior wilderness.

A recipient in 1981 of the Literature Award bestowed by
the American Academy and Institute of Arts and Letters,
Howard Frank Mosher lives with his wife and family near
the Canadian border in Vermont. His writings include
Disappearances, Where the Rivers Flow North, and *Marie
Blythe*.

The Penguin Nature Library

SONGS OF THE NORTH

SIGURD F. OLSON

Edited with an Introduction by
Howard Frank Mosher

Penguin Books

PENGUIN BOOKS
Viking Penguin Inc., 40 West 23rd Street,
New York, New York 10010, U.S.A.
Penguin Books Ltd, 27 Wrights Lane, London W8 5TZ
(Publishing & Editorial), and Harmondsworth, Middlesex,
England (Distribution & Warehouse)
Penguin Books Australia Ltd, Ringwood,
Victoria, Australia
Penguin Books Canada Limited, 2801 John Street,
Markham, Ontario, Canada L3R 1B4
Penguin Books (N.Z.) Ltd, 182–190 Wairau Road,
Auckland 10, New Zealand

First published in Penguin Books 1987
Published simultaneously in Canada

The essays in this collection are selected from six books by Sigurd F. Olson
and are published by arrangement with Alfred A. Knopf, Inc., as follows:
"Athabasca Brigade," "The Red Cliffs of Amisk," and "Father Moraud,"
from *The Lonely Land*. Copyright © 1961 by Sigurd F. Olson.
"Stream of the Past," "Song of the North," "The Maker of Dreams," and
"Beyond the Ranges," from *Open Horizons*. Copyright © 1969 by Sigurd
F. Olson.
"Laughing Loon," "King's Point," and "The Portage," from *Listening
Point*. Copyright © 1958 by Sigurd F. Olson.
"Ghost Camps of the North," "Fond du Lac," and "Spell of the Yukon,"
from *Runes of the North*. Copyright © 1963 by Sigurd F. Olson.
"Campfires," "Pine Knots," "Northern Lights," "Timber Wolves," "Flying
In," and "The Way of a Canoe," from *The Singing Wilderness*. Copyright
© 1945, 1948, 1951, 1955, 1956 by Sigurd F. Olson.
"The Feel of Spring," from *Wilderness Songs*. Copyright © 1956, 1958,
1961, 1963, 1969, 1971 by Sigurd F. Olson.

The illustrations appearing on the first page of each essay are
from the books by Sigurd F. Olson as described above.

Cataloging in Publication data available
ISBN 0 14 01.7007 3

Printed in the United States of America by
R. R. Donnelley & Sons Company, Harrisonburg, Virginia
Set in Janson Linotype

THE PENGUIN NATURE LIBRARY

Nature is our widest home. It includes the oceans that provide our rain, the trees that give us air to breathe, the ancestral habitats we shared with countless kinds of animals that now exist only by our sufferance or under our heel.

Until quite recently, indeed (as such things go), the whole world was a wilderness in which mankind lived as cannily as deer, overmastering with spears or snares even their woodsmanship and that of other creatures, finding a path wherever wildlife could go. Nature was the central theater of life for everybody's ancestors, not a hideaway where people went to rest and recharge after a hard stint in an urban or suburban arena, and many of us still do swim, hike, fish, birdwatch, sleep on the ground, or paddle a boat on vacation, and will loll like a lizard in the sun any other chance we have. We can't help grinning for at least a moment at the sight of surf, or sunlight on a river meadow, as if remembering in our mind's eye paleolithic pleasures in a home before memories officially began.

It is a thoughtless grin because nature predates "thought." Aristotle was a naturalist, and, nearer to our own time, Darwin and Thoreau made of the close observation of bits of nature a lever to examine life in many ways on a large scale. Yet naturewriting, despite its basis in science, usually rings with rhapsody as well—a belief that nature is an expression of God.

In this series we are presenting some nature writers of the past century or so, though leaving out great novelists like Turgenev, Melville, Conrad, and Faulkner, who were masters of natural description, and poets such as Homer (who was perhaps the first nature writer, once his words had been transcribed). Nature writing now combines rhapsody with science and connects science with rhapsody. For that reason it is a very special and a nourishing genre.

—Edward Hoagland

CONTENTS

INTRODUCTION

HOWARD FRANK MOSHER

"THE SONG OF THE NORTH STILL FILLS ME WITH THE SAME GLAD-ness as when I heard it first," Sigurd Olson wrote in the middle of his long and distinguished career as a nature essayist. "More than the terrain, more than the woods, lakes, and forests, it had promise and meaning and sang of the freedom and challenge of the wilderness. I seemed drawn in its general direction as naturally as a migrating bird is by unseen lines of force, or as a salmon by some invisible power toward the stream where it was spawned. Within me was a constant longing, and when I listened to this song, I understood."

It was a song Olson had listened to from his early boyhood in northern Wisconsin. In his first book, *The Singing Wilderness*, he recalls the exact moment he heard it for the first time. Waking at night to the distant moans of foghorns and steamer whistles on Lake Michigan, he felt a sudden, overwhelming urge to see the lake himself, despite gruesome local tales of the ferocious lynx and wildcats infesting the nearby woods. Just seven years old, he set out alone the following morning. He ran most of the way, emerging at last on a wild and lovely scene of crying gulls, crashing waves and the vast blue expanse of the lake. "That day I entered into a life of indescribable beauty and delight," he would later write. "There I believe I heard the singing wilderness for the first time."

This wonderful spirit of adventure, combined with a nearly mystical sense of well-being in any unspoiled natural setting, shaped the course of Olson's entire life. By temperament and upbringing a remarkably serene man, he returned to the wilderness again and again over the years to renew his natural equanimity. Part frontiersman on the last great northern frontier of America, part poet and philosopher, and a fierce preservationist long before the term was coined, Sigurd Olson never lost his sense of wonder and delight in the presence of wild places and wild things.

From the scores of articles and essays Olson wrote, I have selected twenty for this volume. In general, they fall into three overlapping categories. First are three autobiographical accounts chronicling the critical personal and professional junctures in Olson's life. "Song of the North," "Beyond the Ranges," and "The Maker of Dreams" are candid, intensely personal (but never self-indulgent) accounts of Sigurd Olson's decisions to teach, guide, and write in and about his beloved north country. In a different vein, "Athabasca Brigade," "Father Moraud," and "The Red Cliffs of Amisk" recount Olson's canoeing explorations in the northern bush; these marvelous, true narratives of wilderness journeys are reminiscent of Thoreau's *The Maine Woods* and Edward Abbey's *Desert Solitaire*. Finally, *Songs of the North* concludes with a number of Olson's short, interpretive nature pieces garnered from a lifetime of close observation and appreciation of uniquely northern phenomena; these include "Pine Knots," "Northern Lights," and "The Way of a Canoe." Taken together, the following essays reflect the serenity and positivism of Sigurd Olson the man, his passionate vision as a preservationist, and his range, power, and lyricism as a nature writer.

From the start, Olson was irresistibly attracted to the big lake where he first heard the song of the north, and to the vast woods along its shores. Over the course of his boyhood he taught himself to fish for brook trout, to hunt grouse, ducks, and deer, to identify the trees and wildflowers and rugged geologic formations he wrote about so eloquently in later years. As a teenager he grubbed stumps out of swampy pastures on backcountry farms to save money for college. Yet so far as his father, a Baptist minister, was concerned, young

Sig had only three options for a career: farming, teaching, or the ministry.

At the University of Wisconsin, Olson missed the north country terribly, and agonized over his narrow choice of a profession. But as he gradually became immersed in his natural science studies, it seemed to him that teaching "somewhere in the north and near the woods" might be the ideal solution to his dilemma. After a one-year job at a high school in the Mesabi Iron Range of northern Minnesota, and a stint in graduate school, Olson accepted a post teaching biology and geology at Ely Junior College, on the edge of the wild Quetico-Superior border country. It was to be his home for the rest of his life.

As a teacher, Olson liked nothing better than to pack his students off to a remote quaking bog, a flooding spring river full of spawning pike, an abandoned gold mine. Fieldwork, he believed, was the best way to learn, and these tramps through the bush suited his vigorous personal style better than lecturing, though he could explain the scientific causes of sunspots or the northern lights as clearly and simply as he retold a fishing or hunting anecdote from one of the old-time wilderness guides he'd met in his travels. Nor was teaching Olson's only interest. Between semesters, he worked as a guide himself, earning an important supplementary income and, better yet, acquiring extensive first-hand experience in the wilderness.

During the 1920s and '30s, the Quetico-Superior border territory was still a primitive and lovely land of deep icy lakes, unmapped streams, and thick forests inhabited by wolves. Here, as he recounts in "Beyond the Ranges," Olson absorbed skills and lore not taught in college and graduate schools. By watching veteran woodsmen like Buck Sletton, Arnie the Finn, and the ex-lumberjack Gunder Graves, who guided in his "highwater pants" and "Jefferson Drivers" hobnailed boots, he learned how to locate various game fish; to paddle a canoe all day without tiring by utilizing his entire upper body, not just his arms; to portage between lakes using the ancient "*posé*" method of the voyageurs—carrying a load part way, then returning for another before going on, in order to rest on the way back. He quickly picked up the vivid bush lingo: a pack was never a pack, but a "Duluth"; a starting point was a "jumping-off place"; rapids, if they were violent enough, were "white horses." On these early explorations, he honed his appreciation not only for the songs of the wilderness but for its silences and quality of timelessness. For weeks on end, his routine was regulated by the sunrise and sunset, the wind and rain, and his own instincts and inclinations. Best of all, he learned to value "the complete naturalness of living out of doors," which would become a recurrent and powerful theme in his writings.

Olson did not set out at an early age to become a writer. Like teaching and guiding, his essays were a natural outgrowth of his love of wild places. In "The Maker of Dreams," perhaps his most personal essay, he describes his quest to find "a medium of expression beyond teaching . . . that would give life and substance to thoughts and memories, a way of recapturing and sharing again the experiences that were mine." One gray fall evening, on the way home from a long, soul-searching sojourn in the woods, an inspiration came to him. He would capture and transmit the songs of the north by writing about them.

As preparation for this major undertaking, he began to read voraciously: Thoreau, Whitman, Hemingway; William Henry Drummond, "the bard of the fur trade"; and the diaries of the great explorers David Thompson and Alexander Mackenzie. Next came the painstakingly slow business of copious note-taking, numberless false starts, frustrating rejections. After weathering these usual initial setbacks much the way he weathered those first lonely years at college, Olson began writing features for a midwestern newspaper syndicate. In time he enlarged his early vignettes into more comprehensive essays similar in form and content to those of Aldo Leopold, whom he knew and admired. An indefatigable reviser, he learned to avoid the subjunctive mood and awkward inversions of his apprentice work. Like a good white-water canoeist, he never strove to go beyond his expertise, but wrote almost exclusively of the natural world he understood so well. Dozens of his celebratory nature essays are clear, simply eloquent, and informed by his intensely personal relationship with the wilderness, which he came to regard not only as restorative and lovely but essential to the spiritual well-being of human beings.

Like Leopold, Olson frequently used a simple image to suggest a great sweep of natural and human history. Happening across the last remains of a giant fallen pine, he wrote: "That pine was a sapling when the first voyageurs came through on their trading-expeditions some three hundred years ago, was well grown at the time of the American Revolution, crashed to earth during some storm before the loggers moved in sixty years ago. There it lay while the younger pines around it were harvested, and disintegrated slowly as the birch came in. Its knots survived a great fire that swept the area as an aftermath of the logging, lying there hidden beneath the duff and away from the heat . . . that pine knot was a concentration not only of energy but of the country itself. Burning it was the climax not only to its growth but to the expedition on which I found it."

Just as frequently, Olson began an essay by describing a personal experience. During his lifetime in the wilderness, he saw his share of strange and wonderful sights: a weasel borne aloft by the grouse it had fastened onto; a playful mouse scaling his tent roof repeatedly in order to enjoy the exhilarating slide back down the sloped canvas; a mother otter systematically catching baby fish ducks for her own young. He liked facts, found satisfaction in reporting that otters are the fastest swimming mammals, but was equally pleased to note that of all northern animals the otter was "blessed with the most spirit and personality." There was more than a touch of romantic mysticism about him; when an old woodsman crony of Scottish-Cree descent claimed he had actually heard echoes of the songs of the voyageurs who long ago passed through the Quetico territory on fur-trading expeditions,

Olson tried to hear them too, convinced that people who had "lived close to nature all of their lives [were] sensitive to many things lost to those in cities."

Throughout his life, the voyageurs held a special, haunting fascination for Olson. "Each spring at the breakup of ice on the St. Lawrence, great brigades of canoes left Montreal for the west, hundreds of gay and colorful craft fashioned from birch bark, cedar, and spruce," he wrote of those tireless adventurers. "Decorated in gaudy designs, each brigade with its own insignia, vermillion-tipped paddles moving in rhythm to the *chansons* of Old France, here was a pageant such as the New World had never known and will never see again." These wiry French Canadian explorers, who paddled sixteen to eighteen hours a day, slept wrapped in a single blanket under their overturned canoes, and routinely carried 180-pound fur packs along portages at a trot, were Olson's heroes; over the years he retraced their entire 3,500-mile route from Montreal to the Canadian Northwest.

Of all of Olson's books, my favorite is *The Lonely Land*, an account of his 500-mile canoe expedition along the Churchill River in primitive northern Saskatchewan. "There are few places left on the North American continent where men can still see the country as it was before Europeans came and know some of the challenges and freedoms of those who saw it first," this superb narrative of a white water wilderness adventure begins, "but in the Canadian Northwest it can still be done."

With Olson as the "bourgeois," or leader (and cook), he

and a party of five other explorers had the trip of a lifetime. Accurately, enthusiastically, eloquently, he records what his tiny band saw, from great white pelicans to ancient Indian pictographs; whom they met—the resilient Father Moraud, a symbol of the North in a black robe and paint-stained jeans is the most memorable; where and how they camped; the "white horses" they shot, and those they prudently did not.

The Lonely Land reads like exciting fiction with Olson as the main character. Here, even more than in his early autobiographical essays, his love of adventure, his serenity in wild settings, and his naturally positive outlook are apparent on every page. Through his descriptions of the daily routines of breaking camp, planning the day's run, watching the weather, preparing meals, and delegating other tasks, he provides us with a unique, unself-conscious profile of his even-handed leadership; his cheerful endurance under the rigors of traveling twenty or thirty miles a day through some of the most demanding terrain on earth; his boundless capacity to revel in the harshnesses as well as the beauty of the northern wilderness; and his unfailing appreciation of the companionship of his fellow travelers. *The Lonely Land* also affords us a rare glimpse of Olson's personal tastes and idiosyncrasies. He expresses annoyance with a member of the party who occasionally second-guesses his judgment in picking the route. He displays a playful sense of humor, addressing his crew in a mock-solemn Canadian voyageur's dialect. He looks forward to a stiff jolt of rum at the end of a tough day's trek. He searches for campsites on pink granite, facing the sunset, and repeatedly expresses his delight in wild northern names like Flin Flon and the Maligne River, "which spoke of romance, mystery, challenge."

Later in his career, Olson ranged out still further in pursuit of that elusive song of the north, to Great Slave Lake and Great Bear Lake and the Yukon and Alaska; but I think he never had a greater wilderness experience than that trek down the Churchill River, which he exuberantly summarized as "a daily succession of adventures of the spirit."

In the spirit of the nineteenth-century transcendentalists, Sigurd Olson wrote with intense conviction of our "ancient ties to the earth." He saw mankind as part of nature, not so very long ago regulated by the seasons and other natural forces from which he felt we should not "sever our spiritual roots." When, in his later books, he wrote of "the ecologic crisis that threatens our survival," he was speaking quite literally. "We must develop a philosophy which considers the great imponderables, the ancient code of ethics embodying man's sense of oneness and dependence on nature," he stated in his essay "Landscape of the Universe," which best summarizes his personal philosophy of man's interdependence with the wilderness.

Throughout his career, Olson fought tirelessly to defend and preserve the wild land where, for centuries, men and women had gone to renew their sense of oneness with nature. As his long-time friend, Frank Graham, wrote in a profile of Olson in *Audubon* magazine (Nov. 1980), Olson led the successful battle to establish the Superior Primitive Area. Some years later, Olson was instrumental in forming the Quetico-Superior Council, which blocked an attempt to dam and flood out a vast tract of wild country on both sides of the border. In 1947, with the support of his wife, Elizabeth, he resigned from his job as dean of Ely Junior College to devote all his time to writing and to preservationist causes.

Olson went on to serve as a consultant to the Secretary of the Interior, the National Park Service, and the Izaak Walton League of America, as well as activist president of the Wilderness Society and the National Parks Association. Yet this remarkable man continued to find time to write and to return again and again to the wild country near his Minnesota home and far to the north. His legacy was rich and varied: the great expanses of wilderness he fought to preserve from development; the still vaster tracts he preserved in his splendid celebratory prose. As a writer he was at his very best, I believe, chronicling his personal experiences in remote places, which he described so well that his readers share the wonderful sense of well-being he found there. If his vision never seems as powerfully distilled as Aldo Leopold's or Rachel Carson's, his range of subjects was as wide as theirs or wider; and the vast majority of his work far transcends the genre of conventional nature writing.

"This way of existence, living in tents and traveling together each day, seemed the way life should be," Sigurd Olson wrote in *The Lonely Land*. The same could be said of Olson's entire career, from teacher to guide to writer to preservationist. It was a joyful and felicitous union of vocation and avocation. No twentieth-century writer I know of ever combined the two better.

FROM

THE LONELY LAND

CHAPTER I

ATHABASCA BRIGADE

Norway House, 16the August 1820

TO WM. WILLIAMS ESQRE.,
Governor in Chief of Ruperts Land

SIR:

 I HAVE *the Honor to acquaint you that the Athabasca and Peace River Brigades took their departure from hence yesterday morning; much time has been lost from the want of proper subordination amongst the people, and it is with the utmost difficulty we have been enabled to bring them to their duty, they now however promise well and the Guides assure me they will make up for the delay that has taken place. . . . Our Compliment is twelve canoes navigated by sixty men, contg. two hundred and fifty four pieces, which I suspect is far short of what the Department requires, we must make the most of everything, and as Isle à la*

*Crosse is overstocked with goods, I expect Mr. Clarke will fur-
nish us with a supply of such articles as we stand most in need of
during the winter.*

—GEORGE SIMPSON

I WAS UP before the east began to glow and in the half light of
dawn stood down at the beach watching the whitecaps racing
past the point and rolling on toward the north. There was a
tail wind, and the day would be good. We should be at the head
of the lake by late afternoon. What luck, for if the wind had
been against us we would have to fight our way down that
long unbroken stretch toward Patuanak and the Drum. We
could easily have been wind-bound and forced to spend precious hours waiting for a break.

I gathered long shreds of birchbark from a broken tree and
driftwood tossed up by the waves of some previous storm. It
was tinder-dry, for it had been in the sun and the winds had
blown over it as it lay high on the sands. Soon a bright fire was
crackling under the grill. The pots went on and breakfast was
underway, not exactly a voyageur's repast, for we were still
close enough to civilization to enjoy fresh eggs and back bacon, canned fruit, and what was left of the loaf of fresh bread.
While I made everything ready, the tents came down and all
the packing was done except the food and cooking outfit.

As we ate, some of the birds came back screaming in protest

and landed, only to take off again. The pelicans soared over us, then disappeared down the lake. The terns and gulls circled and dipped. Only the shorebirds ran up and down the sand following the ebb and flow of the waves as though we we were not there.

"The pelicans don't like us," said Denis. "Did you see their expressions? For all the world like looking at us over the tops of their spectacles."

I laughed. "They seem to take a dim view of our entire operation. The canoes are too new, our backs the wrong color, and we've disrupted their feeding."

"Give us time," he said. "A few more days and we'll fit into the scenery like the Crees themselves."

We cleaned up the cooking outfit, packed it away, put out the fire, stowed the packs in the canoes and made a final check of the tent sites. Everything was in order. We stood at the water's edge ready to take off.

"Thirty miles to go," announced Omond, after consulting his map. "With this gale we should make the end of the lake by nightfall."

Ile à la Crosse was important in the old days. Everyone came through who traveled into the Northwest. Down this broad stretch the canoes had headed for Athabasca and the Mackenzie; to Ile à la Crosse had come the brigades from Saskatchewan to the south. Here was a crossroads of travel as well-known in the West as Grand Portage on Lake Superior.

Mackenzie made these notations coming through upstream:

"Then Shagoina strait and rapid lead into the Lake of Ile à la Crosse, in which the course is south twenty miles, and south-south-west fourteen miles, to the Point au Sable; opposite to which is the discharge of the Beaver-River, bearing south six miles; the lake in the distance run does not exceed twelve miles in its greatest breadth. It now turns west-south-west, the Isle à la Crosse being on the south, and the mainland on the north; and it clears the one and the other in the distance of three miles, the water presenting an open horizon to right and left; that on the left formed by a deep narrow bay, about ten leagues in depth; and that to the right by what is called la Riviere Creuse, or Deep River, being a canal of still water which is here four miles wide. On following the last course, Isle à la Crosse Fort appears on a low isthmus, at the distance of five miles, and it is in latitude 55.25. North, and longitude 107. West."

Our canoes were birchbarks that morning, freshly gummed for the rapids and waves ahead, my partners voyageurs, bronzed, bearded, and burned from wintering in the Athabasca country. They were on their way to Grand Portage to meet old friends, to eat fresh bread again, to dance to the fiddles in the Great Hall, to fight heroic battles on the beach and to do the things they could boast about for a year to come.

We had plenty of freeboard and as we began to ride the swells from the south, feeling the lift and power of them, the men of the old brigades rode with us. That morning there were songs in the wind: *En roulant ma boule, La Belle Lizette, La Claire Fontaine*. In the sound of the rising wind we could hear them.

En roulant ma boule roulant,
En roulant ma boule
En roulant ma boule roulant
En roulant ma boule.

The steady rhythm became part of my own stroke and unconsciously I followed the pace they set. Suddenly Denis began to sing the favorite chanson of all voyageurs:

"A la claire fontaine
M'en allant promener,
J'ai trouvé l'eau si belle
Que je m'y suis bangné.
Lui ya longtemps que je t'aime,
Jamais je ne t'oublierai."

The others joined in and as we paddled down the lake, more than ever we became a part of the ancient scene. The vistas were the same, the promontories, the new moon paling behind us, the sparkling waves, the wild crying of gulls and terns. This was the Northwest, this part of the long trail we had begun the summer before.

Our three canoes were almost abreast now, no more than a stone's throw apart. Each time a long roller came they lifted, poised for a moment, slipped down into the trough, only to rise again. Peterborough Prospectors were made for days like this. With the gale behind them, they were making better than four miles an hour, possibly five or even six if the wind held. Suddenly our canoe lifted higher than before and we hung poised on a white hissing comber. As we slipped downward into the trough, spray covered the canoe and Denis flinched as the cold water struck his bare back.

"Bourgeois," he yelled, "I used to feel that on the bridge but then I had my oilskins on."

I looked around for the other canoes. No longer abreast, at times they all but disappeared and were hidden by spray. From the vantage point of a canoe riding with a gale, the lives we had known seemed strangely remote. Within a matter of a day and a night, a change had come to all of us, a change no one noticed at the time because it was so natural. This we knew from long experience was one of the great compensations of all wilderness expeditions. What was important was that we were heading down the historic trail of Alexander Mackenzie by canoe, that the wind was in our favor and that there was a chance for a camp that night at the far end of the lake. The future to us was Drum Rapids, Deer, and Leaf and many fast waters that had no names.

A little rocky island ahead seemed to be covered with white and had it been late fall we would have guessed it was a mantle of snow. As we neared however, we saw it was completely hidden by the closely packed bodies of pelicans, so close together that nowhere did the rocks show through. Suddenly the far edge of the mantle began to lift and peeled off slowly to the other end. For a moment sunlight glittered on a milling confusion of snowy wings, and then the great birds took off in sedate formation toward the far shore.

Two of them left the main flock and soared toward us

wing tip to wing tip as perfectly co-ordinated in their movements as veteran pilots maneuvering together. They flew directly over us once and then again and seemingly satisfied with their reconnaissance, soared back to the flock which was resting some distance ahead.

Four hours later and possibly twenty miles from our starting point there was a slight shift in the wind, a barely perceptible shift at first, an indefinite quartering as though it could not quite make up its mind what to do. At first I thought it might be due to its veering around an island or a point, but gradually its direction changed until it was almost broadside. We watched with apprehension, hoping it was only a temporary diversion or a swirl which would finally settle down into the steady wind we had coasted with that far. More and more it swung. Rounding a sharp promontory, we found that long, uneasy swells were moving against us. Before we had gone a mile, those swells became waves with whitecaps and we knew our work was cut out for us. Still more than ten miles to go and if we were to maintain our schedule, we would have to fight every foot of the way.

We stopped for our noon snack in the lee of a small boulder-strewn island, feasted on hardtack, summer sausage, and cheese, and washed it down with a drink of lemonade. This was topped with a handful of raisins and a square of hard chocolate. As we sat munching our rations, the waves grew steadily higher. Omond checked his chart carefully.

"About ten miles of fighting the wind," he said. "We'll hug the east shore and take advantage of what cover there is."

"Let's go," I said, as soon as the lunch pack was stowed in my canoe. "In another hour this island will be awash." Already some of the biggest waves were covering us with spray.

All afternoon we fought the waves, dodged behind points and islands and any features of the shoreline that gave us protection. What a beating birchbark canoes would have taken on such a day! Seams would have needed calking to stop the trickles coming through, and packs might have become wet. With canvas canoes we had no worry, and the Peterboroughs rode the biggest waves without shipping a drop. Instead of making four or five miles an hour, however, we were now slowed to a pace of two or less.

We could have hired an Indian with a motor-driven canoe and covered the ground in half the time, and for a moment as I watched the canoes battling their way down the storm-tossed lake I wondered if we had been wise. But I knew if we had taken a tow we would have lost what we had come to find— the feeling of a great waterway and the men who traversed it long before our time. Theirs was a slow pace with time to absorb the terrain itself, its smells and sights and sounds, the intangible impressions that come only when a man moves slowly under his own power across the face of the earth. Like them, we were a brigade moving toward Cumberland House.

At last we saw the dim outlines of the low shore at the end of the lake, a swampy expanse where it turned toward Lake Shagwenaw and our second camp. For three hours more we paddled desperately and then hove to in the protection of a final point. There we turned and looked for the last time down the forty-mile stretch of Ile à la Crosse. We were weary, ready to make camp anywhere, but still had several miles to go. Hugging the shore we turned east into the swift channel of a narrows, ran our first rapids.

The smooth current emptied into the lake. There before us was the little Indian settlement of Patuanak, the thin white spire of a tiny church, the clustered shacks, tents and fish-drying racks of another Cree community. The dogs howled long before we were near, a sound that was to become so much a part of the Lonely Land that never again would we hear it without thinking of the Churchill. While we had known we would find the village and its mission, somehow it seemed incongruous to have them materialize. This was particularly true of the church, even though it was now as much a part of the life of this waterway as the Hudson's Bay Posts themselves. As we neared, we could see the bright red flag over the company store and the freshly painted house of the clerk set back of the compound. We pushed into the dock, were met by a crowd of curious children, several women and older people, and one who looked like a dwarf.

They looked at us in amazement. It was a strange thing for white men to be paddling canoes. Everyone used large freighters and motors. Even the poorest Indian wanted some sort of mechanized transport. The canoe might be broken and patched, the motor of ancient vintage, held together with wire and rope and bits of tin, but at least it meant he didn't have to paddle. Paddling was for fishing off the major waterways, for women and children and muskrat trappers, certainly not for major expeditions down the Churchill. It was inconceivable anyone would travel this way for pleasure.

Our pack sacks were interesting to them for since the days of the old brigades most carrying had been done by the time-honored method of a tump line and harness. The tump line itself is merely a broad leather strap from which extend several long thongs. The article to be carried is usually wrapped in a tarpaulin, tied with the thongs, the actual carrying being done with the strap across the forehead. If the first bundle fits neatly against the small of the back, other pieces can be placed on top, and the weight will rest on the back and shoulders, with the real strain on the head.

This was the way voyageurs carried their standard load of two *pièces*, or 180 pounds, and they spoke with awe of some who had carried five and even eight at one time. The tradition continues, for Paul Provencher speaks of one "Harry Pitlegans, a Montagnais half-breed who on a bet in 1927 carried over six hundred pounds of flour ankle deep in soft sand for a quarter of a mile."

All of this had always been done with the tump line and harness, and the Indians knew its history. No wonder they looked at our packs with astonishment. True they also had a head strap, but the actual carrying was done with shoulder straps. Mackenzie, when speaking of transporting goods across the nine miles of Grand Portage, paid the voyageur a high compliment when he said:

"When they arrived at Grand Portage, which is near nine miles over, each of them had to carry eight packages of such goods and provisions as are necessary for the interior country. This is a labor which cattle cannot conveniently perform in summer as both horses and oxen were tried by the company without success."

Of greatest interest was my pack basket in which I carried lunches, a lightweight woven box of red-pine strips built to fit snugly into one of the packs and stiff enough so that bannock, eggs, jam, or any breakables could be carried safely. In that basket went the tea pail, six cups, salt and pepper and the snacks we would need for the noon meal. The Indians had known the grub box but they had never seen a device like this. Both served the same purpose, did away with the necessity of searching for items of food or undoing a regular pack during the day. When the time came to eat, only that one box or pack had to be undone. It always rode in my canoe and no one else carried it.

One look at the cluttered shoreline and the ravenous dogs, and we decided not to stop. Even though the shores beyond looked low and swampy there must be some place better than the village. I wanted to go to the post, however, to exchange some of our unsmoked Canadian back bacon—which an unknowing clerk had decided we needed—for the heavily smoked bush variety. There is little fat on back bacon and we knew that within a week, being uncured, it would become tainted. So we laid in a supply of the brown boardlike slabs which would keep indefinitely, no matter what the weather.

Back again at the dock we asked the dwarf, who was very talkative, about the Indian known as Wolverine whom we had been told knew more about the river than anyone else.

"He fly away," said the dwarf, "far, far away." And he pointed to the east. "Two days ago he fly."

We had been told at Ile à la Crosse that a fire was raging somewhere beyond Primeau and we knew a government plane had come in and picked up a crew. When I asked about a camping place, he said: "Good camp on beach."

"What about a rocky place?" I asked.

He laughed. "No stones, no stones any place. Why?"

The answer to that simple question was far too difficult and involved for me to attempt a reply. All I said was: "We like rocks better than swamp and trees."

I knew that did not make much of an impression. It was beyond them why we did not go down to the beach and camp back of the rushes or pitch our tents right where we were like everyone else. Crazy white men paddling canoes, funny pack sacks and queer notions about where to stop for the night.

The voyageurs of the old brigades would not have scorned the village and the post, and no doubt they had stopped there many times in the past. Husky dogs, thieving children, flies and dirt and noise would not have disturbed them in the least. They would have turned over their big birchbark canoes, built a fire near the shore and made merry with the Indians, but then their needs had been somewhat different from ours. While we sought to escape even little native settlements and be as much on our own as possible, to them any sort of a gathering after their long and arduous travels was a welcome relief from loneliness and monotony.

CHAPTER II

THE RED CLIFFS OF AMISK

THE *Sturgeon Weir River discharges itself into this lake, and its bed seems to be of the same kind of rock, and is almost a continual rapid. Its direct course is almost west by north, and with its windings is about thirty miles. It takes its waters into Beaver Lake [Amisk], the southwest side of which consists of the same rock lying in thin strata; the route then proceeds from island to island for about twelve miles, and along the north shore, for four miles more, the whole being a northwest course to the entrance of the river in latitude 54.32. North.*

—ALEXANDER MACKENZIE

THE NEXT MORNING we awakened to the drum of rain on our tents. The wind had been from the west, blowing directly into our shelters, and the ends of the sleeping bags were drenched. I leaned over and felt mine, then Tony's. Both were sodden and heavy. They would have to dry for a long time in sun and wind before they would be light and fluffy again. Slipping on my rain shirt, I went outside to start the fire, but every time a blaze started the wind and rain put it out. After many tries I succeeded, and when the coffee had come to a boil and the mush was cooked, I called the rest. We sat there in the shelter of the Baker-tent fly, no one saying much except Tony.

"Did you notice, Bourgeois," he asked me in his delectable accent, "those poodles in the tent?"

It was just what we needed. "We had the biggest poodles," said Elliot laughing, "a whole litter of them from one end of the tent to the other."

Only Eric had escaped, for he had been able to pitch his little tent at enough of an angle to the shelf to miss the rain.

It seemed foolhardy to start out in such weather, and we waited hopefully for a break that never came. Finally we packed the wet tents, the soggy bags, and the outfit into the canoes and drifted down toward the portage.

In the rain, Leaf Rapids sounded even louder than the night before. The landing was slippery and the portage still white with hailstones. In the hollows were mounds of them, and we scooped them up with our hands. Slipping and sliding, trying to watch our footing, we made the carry without mishap, loaded the canoes once more, and headed down toward Scoop Rapids. There, according to the Crees, travelers could always dip out a fish from a shallow pool at the lower end. Someone long ago, they said, had left a scoop net there for that purpose, each user leaving it in the same place for the next one coming through. We did not find the scoop, nor did we locate the pool, for the rapids were roaring and high and the fishing place covered by the flood.

"Perhaps," said Denis, "the little men have taken it away, the ones with no noses."

It was there we met Conservation Officer Charley Salt camped all alone at the portage's upper end, high above the landing. He had come up the river with his motor, told us of a broken Grumman canoe below Snake Rapids, advised us strongly not to try running them. A husky young lad from eastern Ontario, he had taken to the bush as naturally as an Indian. Broad of shoulder, with flashing white teeth, an open face and a shock of long blond hair, he looked like a Viking. His neat little tent was pitched tight as a fiddlestring, and his whole outfit was spanking new and clean.

To Charley Salt, traveling alone to Pelican Rapids, the North was still all romance and excitement, every difficulty a challenge, every hardship savored to the full. We watched him pack and head toward Leaf and the Maligne, caught his gay wave as he disappeared around the bend.

Beyond Scoop there was swamp again, with a profusion of

bird life. We passed an Indian cemetery on the north bank of the river and saw several lob pines marking the course and its many turns. Lob pines are the original trail markers of voyageur days. Picking a spruce or small pine on some high ridge or promontory, voyageurs stripped branches from the lower part of the tree, leaving a tuft or broom on top. Sometimes they merely cut a section from beneath the tip. But whatever the method employed, such a tree could be seen for long distances. Travelers accustomed to watching the skyline with its evenly pinnacled fringe of spruce would notice immediately any discrepancy. In the old days lob pines marked the canoe routes from Montreal into the far Northwest. It was good to see them again, to realize there were still places where such old traditions survive, even in the jet age.

As we paddled along I thought of what Charley Salt had said about the new fish-filleting plant at Pelican Narrows. Planes were coming in daily during the fishing season to fly the fillets to Winnipeg for shipment to the East. A new wave of prosperity was dawning for the Indians, and their old way of life was changing fast. As I watched a lone lob pine on the horizon, I wondered if the changes would bring as much happiness as he thought.

Signs of beaver were plentiful, indicating there was little trapping on the river. Along the Churchill there had been none at all, except up tributary creeks; now there was evidence everywhere. Whitened sticks of gnawed aspen floated along the shore. There were signs on trails and canals leading inland. Flattened sedges showed where they had been. Perhaps, I thought, the fishing industry was keeping trappers close at home, resulting in the abandonment of ancient trapping grounds. In time, perhaps, the beaver might even move close to the villages, if no one was interested in the hard work of taking them.

All that day, beavers were with us. It seemed right to be in beaver country again, for of all forms of life in the Northwest, this animal was responsible for exploration and trade. A beaver skin was standard currency and all articles of trade were evaluated by the number of skins they would bring.

A Moose Fort Record of 1784 gave a few comparative trading values.

Arrowheads	9	1	Beaver
Awl blades	12	1	"
Bayonets	2	1	"
Beads	1 #	2	"
Bells hawk	8 prs.	1	"
Blankets	1 point	1	"
Blankets	2 points	2½	"
Blankets	3 points	4	"
Boxes tobacco	2	1	"
Brandy	1 Gns	4	"
Buttons	12 doz.	1	"
Cloth	1 yd	2	"
Chizzels	2	1	"
Combs	2	1	"
Flints	20	1	"

Guns	4 ft	12 Beaver
Shot	5 #	1 "
Gunpowder	2 Horns	1 "
Kettles	1 #	1 "
Shirts check	1	1 "
Spoons	4	1 "
Knives	8	1 "
Stockings	1 pr	1¼ "

The beaver skin was the standard in evaluating all other furs. It took two of the hides to be worth as much as one wolverine, three for a bear, one for twenty rabbits, 4 mink, or 10 pounds of goose feathers. The beaver was king for almost three hundred years. Today it is revered as a symbol in all of Canada.

While we were paddling by the mouth of a little creek a beaver appeared, swimming across the opening with a leafy branch of aspen in its mouth. When it saw the canoe it raised its tail and with a mighty whack warned all members of the colony to beware.

A little farther on was a house close to the shore, a live house with much activity around it. The beavers were laying in their winter's supply of food and had already sunk a considerable amount of brush, aspen, birch, alder, and willow. Before long the fall storms would come, followed by the swift freezing of all lakes and rivers. Then for six months they would subsist on what they had stored.

"Dose beavaire," said Denis, "she is a mighty fine aneemahl."

Several hours later we approached Snake Rapids Portage, one of the longest we would encounter on our trip down the Weir. We found it immediately, traveled the three quarters of a mile without the usual rests, found at its end the broken aluminum canoe Charley had told us about. It had gone down the rapids, been wedged between two rocks and torn apart by the force of the current. Whose it was or whether or not its owners had come through alive, we did not know. Someone had hauled it onto the rocks and left it there as a reminder of what can happen. We stood around it, looking it over, all of us thinking the same thing. This might well have been one of our Peterboroughs, but the story would then have been different; instead of a torn and twisted piece of metal it would have been a splintered wreck of cedar, spruce, and canvas.

At such a place, where someone had probably drowned, the voyageurs would have erected crosses. Daniel Harmon on an expedition in 1800 out of Montreal toward the West spoke of the effect these markers had on him. Passing Roche Capitaine Portage, he said:

"This portage is so named from a large rock, that rises to a considerable height above the water in the middle of the rapid. During the day, we have come up several difficult ones, where many persons have been drowned, either in coming up or going down. For every such unfortunate person, whether his corpse is found or not, a cross is erected by his companions, agreeably to a custom of the Roman Catholics; and at this place, I see no less than fourteen. This is a melancholy sight. It leads me to reflect on the folly and temerity of man, which causes him to press on in the path, that has conducted so many of his fellow creatures prematurely to the grave. . . .

"The Canadian Voyageurs, when they leave one stream to go up or down another, have a custom of pulling off their hats, and making the sign of the cross, upon which one in each canoe, or at least, in each brigade repeats a short prayer. The same ceremonies are observed by them, whenever they pass a place where someone has been interred, and a cross erected. Those therefore who are in the habit of voyaging this way, are obliged to say their prayers more frequently perhaps than when at home; for at almost every rapid which we have passed, since we left Montreal, we have seen a number of crosses erected; and at one I counted no less than thirty. . . . With such dismal spectacles, however, almost continually before our eyes, we press forward, with all the ardor and rashness of youth, in the same dangerous path, stimulated by the hopes of gratifying the eye and of securing a little gold."

Toward sunset we were at the final rapids above Amisk Lake. This, according to the map, was Spruce, and we looked them over carefully, remembering the Grumman. It was getting late and the channel was far from reassuring, so we decided to be prudent, make the portage and reach Amisk without accident. There we would surely find a good camp site on some island or point. Salt had mentioned several old Indian shacks or "cabooses" as he called them at the opening of the river, but as we approached and saw their dank and swampy situation we gave up the idea of sleeping under a roof and headed for the big water instead.

As we passed beyond the fringing rushes of the river's outlet, there was an open horizon and, several miles across, a long point with limestone cliffs blazing in the level rays of the setting sun. It was as though a great brush had streaked it with Chinese red. Off the Shield once more and before us was the horizontal limestone of another geological era, limestone evidently covered with the same orange lichens we had seen at our second camp on Shangwenaw, transformed again by the blazing sun.

We sat there in our canoes, conscious of the whitecaps out in the open. While it was perfectly calm where we were, half a mile from shore and toward the cliffs a gale was having its way. We must quickly decide either to camp where we were, hug the right shore and travel much farther to reach the outlet, or take advantage of the northwest wind and sail across in an hour.

After all the big water we had been through—Dead Lake, Mirond, and Ile à la Crosse—I knew we could make it. The Peterboroughs could take this one as they had taken blows many times before without shipping so much as a drop; we were seasoned canoemen and knew the score. We would have to work our way around the end of a long point and its shining spray-tossed cliffs and find shelter behind it. Within an hour it would be dusk, but that last hour would be a beautiful one with the wind all but hurling us toward our goal. It was too good a chance to miss, too exciting a challenge to forego.

The canoes came together in the swampy lee of the river's opening and we debated our course. I sensed the voyageurs all felt as I did, confident and sure. The cliffs were flaming brighter than ever. There was no resisting them now.

Omond looked at me. "Bourgeois," he said, "it's up to you."

I looked toward the cliffs once more and the wave-tossed miles in between.

"Let's go," I said, and without more ado we headed out into the open.

The canoes were well spaced but close enough so we would not lose touch. As the distance from the shore increased, we began to feel the wind and were soon in the grip of it, coasting the broad rollers toward the red cliffs.

The wind was steady and the farther out we got the stronger it became, pushing like a great hand on our backs. Hissing combers were around us and it was every canoe for itself, no chance even for a side glance to see what was happening to the others. Carefully quartering to the southeast and toward the end of the point, I was conscious of each wave, judging its power and lift by the sharpness of the approaching hiss. If we skirted the point too close we might hit submerged rocks, if we went out too far we could be carried out into the open lake with its twelve-mile sweep and miss our chance of turning into the shelter behind it.

The cliffs were still a couple of miles away. Only the tip of the point was flaming, the base a dull, angry red fading into the blackness toward the west. The canoe would ride a great roller, slip off its crest, and in that moment of cascading down the slope of the trough we would start quartering. In the blow on Dead Lake the sun had been shining, the combers sparkling and alive. Now in the near dusk they were dull and gray, the valleys in between, bottomless and black. Like running a rapids in poor light, you depended on the feel of things.

Every third or fourth wave was bigger than the rest and I could sense its lift long before it struck. When it caught us the canoe would rise swiftly, then hurtle forward like a great gray spear into the spray. The cliffs were much closer now, their lower parts brushed with black, only the top and very tip of the point still colored. All I could think of was a red knife sticking out into the blackness of the east, its tip alive, its blade and handle darkening into purple. We were quartering successfully and would miss the stiletto's end, but what was in its lee we did not know. Could we land there, or would we find the same precipitous cliffs we faced? We would have to camp there even if we had to climb clear to their tops.

As we drew near, the roar of crashing waves was deafening. Great blocks of limestone lay out in the water below the cliffs with spray dashing high around them. I headed our canoe toward a point a hundred yards beyond the farthest rock lying off the end of the point. Then exactly as we had planned and hoped, we were slipping smoothly by. At that moment there was a slight lull in the wind. I turned the canoe sharply and we were coasting along a calm and beautiful shore covered with flat horizontal slabs of rock backed by huge trees.

In the lee of a limestone block that lay just inside the tip of the point we had a good view of the entire shore. We picked a flat place a few hundred yards below and landed, hauled the canoes out of danger, and found level spots for the tents under big spreading spruces nearby. Denis and I built a fireplace and a patio out of slabs of yellow limestone. There was an abundance of dry wood, and a fire was soon burning and supper under way.

We had found a strange new land. The trees behind us were entirely different from the aspen, spruce, and birch we had known all the way down the Churchill and the Weir. We were off the Shield again and were now on a sedimentary formation that extended far toward Athabasca and the Mackenzie.

Omond fixed a special brew that night and a surprise, some hoarded nuts. We drank to our luck in finding another beautiful camp site and to the red cliffs of Amisk. As we sat there quietly in the dusk listening to the gale roaring harmlessly overhead and the heavy crash of combers off the point, there was little to say about what we had done. But none of us would ever forget the glory of those cliffs flaming in the last rays of the sun, the wind-washed waves with their foaming crests, the sense of being hurled across those miles toward an uncertain goal, and then the calm, with the shouting all behind us.

As I sat there I thought of Al Kennedy, an old prospector friend of mine, who thirty years before had wanted me to come here with him to look for gold. He had been in the rush of the year before and returned with fabulous stories of nuggets and moose and Indian tribes. I was young then and had listened with wide-eyed wonder. Flin Flon—the very sound of it meant adventure. But I did not go after all and stayed in the Quetico-Superior country and the land of the Hudson Bay watershed. I often wondered what might have happened had it been otherwise. Would I have found the gold, or would I have been just another bushwhacker roaming the wilds and searching for the elusive mother lode? We were now within a few miles of Flin Flon, but I would not see it after all.

The Chinese red of the cliffs across the lake was almost gone, fading to mahogany, and the waves were wine and black. Only those close in showed glistening crests. A long slow wash of surf came into our bay. Tomorrow with the wind down, we could cross the open stretch before us, head down the final reaches of the Sturgeon Weir toward Namew and then to Cumberland House where we would say good-by to the canoes, pack our outfit for the last time and go down the great Saskatchewan to The Pas.

CHAPTER III

FATHER MORAUD

It is true my son," said the good old man, "that you will have many monsters to overcome, and precipices to pass in this enterprise, which demands the strength of the most robust. You do not know a word of the language of these nations whom you are going to try and gain to God, but courage, you will gain as many victories as combats."

Advice of FATHER GABRIEL
to FATHER HENNEPIN *on leaving
for explorations in the west* (1678)

THE MORNING DAWNED with a high wind, black scudding rain clouds and squalls that raced across the channel. I went down for a bucket of water and stood looking out over the wild and restless scene. The east was yellow and partly green, with just a rift to show where the sun should be and then it turned to gray and black. Most anything could happen.

Omond joined me. "Eric's temperature is down to normal," he said, "if he takes it easy he can travel."

"We'll break camp then," I answered, "and go as far as we can."

I prepared the usual pot of porridge, a pound of Red River cereal with half a pound of raisins, mixed a batch of fish cakes and made a pot of coffee. Eric ate with us, looking wan, but otherwise none the worse for his ordeal. I thanked him for the layover, promised in return that we would carry him over the portages, if necessary, paddle his canoe, wait upon him all day long. I knew with Eric there would be none of that.

After breakfast we loaded the canoes, skirted the point of the island, and headed into the teeth of the wind across a narrow wave-tossed channel that separated us from the east shore, then worked down the narrows toward the opening into Primeau Lake. The sky grew darker and darker and there was a spattering of rain. Swiftly we got out ponchos to cover the packs and ourselves. Then came a solid lashing wall of rain straight out of the wind, churning the surface of the lake to white. There was no escape as it bore down on us, and we cringed under its impact. The packs, thanks to the ponchos, were dry, but there was now half an inch of water in the bottom of the canoes. We would soon have to land and tip them out before the packs became soaked.

Halfway down the lake the sun came out from behind a cloud. The rain stopped and there were spots of blue. The sky was still threatening but for the moment the storm was over. As we pulled off the ponchos and our rain shirts we heard the roar of a big motor from the west. A freighter canoe rounded a point of land in a plume of spray and bore down directly upon us. We could see a man standing in the bow, a tiny figure in a ski cap, with a white flowing beard and a black robe flying in the wind. When the craft was alongside our little flotilla, it stopped. We paddled close and rested in its lee.

The man was a priest. He told us his name was Moraud and that he had lived in the Churchill River country for over forty years. Denis, who spoke to him in French, discovered he was a brother of the late Senator Moraud of Ottawa and that they had many friends in common. While they chatted on and gesticulated as Frenchmen always do, I sat and studied Father Moraud.

To me he seemed the epitome of all the men of God who had braved the wilderness since the days of early exploration. A small man, hard and wiry and weather-beaten, he stood in the bow of his big canoe, a symbol of the North and of the Church. Here, I thought, might be the spirit of Father Hennepin and all the men of many sects who have given their lives for an ideal, far removed from civilization, from crowds and cities. He like all the rest had deliberately chosen a way of life different from his heritage. What he had chosen must have been adequate compensation for the loss of contact with the culture that made him what he was.

As though to prove it, on his face was written peace and a withdrawal from mundane things. He had known the North for forty years, its vast distances by canoe in the summer, by dog-team and snowshoe during the winters. The howling huskies around the villages, the long white silences and northern lights, times of starvation and disease as well as years of plenty and quiet golden autumns, all this he had known.

Beneath his black spotless robe were paint-stained dungarees. I could see them when the wind blew the cassock wide. The robe he had donned hurriedly when he came to meet us, for it was the symbol of his calling. The dungarees revealed a man of action who scorned no work. To a man of the cloth in the wilderness, menial tasks were necessary, and therefore dignified, being the work of God. He was on his way, he said, to visit someone toward Knee Lake, someone who needed help.

"Come to my cabin and stay the night," he said finally. "There is plenty room and I have food."

We thanked him but refused. We had already lost a day on Dipper Lake.

He left us then and the great canoe roared back into the waves and spray and Father Moraud stood in the bow holding onto the thwart, bouncing up and down with its pitching. The sun was out. We still needed to drain out the water, so we pushed on to a flat rock at the narrows. There we lifted out the packs, turned over the canoes, and laid out the ponchos to dry. After a pot of tea, Omond and Tony took off for Knee Lake, followed by Elliot and Eric. Denis and I busied ourselves with drying out and cleaning the cooking outfit. As we were finishing, the big canoe returned and Father Moraud repeated his invitation.

"Come and stay with me tonight," he called across the waves. "There is plenty room and food."

Again we were forced to refuse and when he saw we were determined to go on, he bowed from the waist, raised his hand in blessing and went back the way he had come.

I shall never forget that gesture from the front of that beaten-up old freight canoe. It was the bow of a courtier who understood our dilemma perfectly and though he wanted us to come, would not press the point. While we stood watching his canoe disappear in the west, we regretted our decision. He could have given us so much of the history of the country, so much of himself that we would never know. I wanted to ask how he felt about the whole Churchill River country, what was going to happen to the Indians, how they felt about the church and the precepts of Christianity and what was happening to their own spirit world. There was so much to learn that only he could tell. Most of all I wanted to know if the hardships and the life in the wilderness had satisfied him completely, if its compensations were great enough to make up for losing Quebec and Montreal and the society of those who were his cultural equals. As I stood there watching the freighter grow smaller and smaller and finally disappear behind a point, I resolved that some day I would come back, spend a week or a month with him, for it might take that long to find the answers to my questions.

But as I paddled away I knew the answers, for Father Moraud felt as Hennepin, Marquette, Allouez, and the host of men of God who since early in 1600 had followed the traders and explorers into the hinterlands. I remembered Louise Hasbrouck's description of Father Hennepin's preparation to accompany La Salle in 1678:

"Upon learning at Quebec of his being chosen to accompany La Salle, Hennepin began at once to make his preparations. These were simple since he took no other garment but that he had on, the grey robe with the rope girdle, and carried in his little bark canoe only a blanket and a rush mat for a bed, and his most precious possession, a portable chapel or box containing an altar and the requisites for saying mass, given him by one of his superiors in Canada. Frontenac, always fond of the Recollet Order dined him at the castle in Quebec, and soon after the friar, with two canoemen, set out on the first stage of his long trip. La Salle was to follow later."

The sun disappeared and the rain began again. Though we paddled off into the teeth of it, we did not leave Father Moraud, for he was with us in spirit. In the short space of a few moments sitting in the lee of his canoe we had met a man who had dedicated himself to an ancient tradition. We would never forget his bearing, the white flowing beard, the jaunty way he wore his cap, the immaculate cassock over stained dungarees. His was the spirit of all the priests who had ever gone into the bush.

"Bourgeois," said Denis, laying his paddle across the bow and turning toward me, "I wished we could have stayed."

"We should have," I said, "but now it is too late."

The rain continued, came down in sheets, and again the canoes were drenched. As we approached Crooked Rapids, a party of Indians bore down on us from the upper lake and stopped at a point ahead to make camp. They looked at us in amusement as we approached, white men paddling canoes and traveling in the rain. Surely we must be mad. What could possibly be so urgent that we must keep going in spite of the weather. We pulled alongside their overturned canoe as they came down to the shore to see what we wanted.

"What about the rapids?" I asked, but they simply shook their heads. Denis tried French with the same result. Gradually we got the impression they were not too bad, that we could run them without danger if we were careful. Our Hudson's Bay Company map said: "If the water is high as at present, go down to left of island with the canoes light. No portage. If water is low, portage on left bank." Again we would have to wait and see. No one seemed exactly sure of what to do.

Simpson met a band of Indians somewhere in this area when he came through in 1820. "Made an early start," he states in his journal, "passed through Knee Lake, made Knee Lake Portage, Decharge de Rapid Croche, and found a band of Ile à la Crosse Indians at Lac Croche, in charge of one Pellant,

A N.W. Servant. . . . Three of Mr. Clarkes Indians were in this band, they complain bitterly that they have no Company's Servant to protect them, Mr. Clarke therefore left one of his people with them, proceeded and met a Half Size Canoe from Isle à la Crosse with supplies for the Indians. The delay and neglect that has taken place in forwarding these supplies arises from the dilatory measures of Mr. Spence who was left in charge of the District for the summer. Got through Lac la Croche and Lac Primeau, made portage la Puisse and encamped at six O'Clock, Raining in torrents."

These quiet, noncommittal Indians were as much a part of the country now as then. Like the caribou and the moose they were indigenous and made little impact on the land. While as yet we had seen none of the animals, we knew they were still around. In the old days, when the caribou migrated, the Indians followed north like wolves to the barrenlands in the summertime, then south to the protecting woods during the months of cold. The great herds of caribou always moved, for only by doing so could they find subsistence. Moss and browse grow slowly in the North and could not survive being eaten constantly. Only by migration over a vast terrain was it possible for caribou to maintain themselves without depletion or exhaustion of their food supplies. So over the hills and ridges the phantom herds would drift, leaving little sign of their presence. The Indians would drift with them until they had taken what they needed and then move back to their villages along the Churchill. The wilderness returned swiftly when they had abandoned their encampments. First, grass and berry bushes, then aspen and willow would appear. And on the rocks the lichens would grow. In a few years no one would know Indians had been there.

By the time we reached the head of the lake it was late afternoon. The other canoes had stopped to give Eric a rest and to wait for us. The rain was over, but we could see no sign of a portage. With the banks in flood, old landings were out of sight, as well as brush that had been beaten down or rocks which had been marked. Denis and I moved down toward the rapids, while the others watched from their precarious positions just above the lip of the first descent. We drew closer and closer. I stood up for a final look. There was no smooth V this time, no channels down between the spouting rocks. The rapids were long and dangerous, with white spouts high and spectacular.

Realizing at the last moment that there was no safe channel anywhere ahead, we turned the canoe sharply to the left, slipped into the willows and then on into flooded birches and hung on to them with the water swirling around us. Foot by foot we pulled ourselves farther into the protection of larger trees and when the water was shallow enough, jumped out and began to wade, pulling the canoe downstream and parallel to the main flow of the river. Ignominious, but safe, it was far better than taking a chance out in the open with the dark closing in. Running strange rapids in sunlight is one thing, but doing it with lowering clouds and bad light is another. In the dusk they seem twice as dangerous.

The other canoes, seeing what we had done, went into the

willows above us, pushed farther into the shore, found an ancient trail choked with brush and windfalls and portaged down to the point where Denis and I finally came out. Drenched once more, partly from the rain, with water sloshing around in the bottom of the canoe, we knew we too would have to land soon to save the packs and their precious contents from getting any wetter than they were. The current was still fast, but we shot the balance of the rapids without difficulty and rounded a bend. There to our joy at the head of another rapids was a broad shelf of pink granite. It looked like a good camp site. We had had enough for one day, went ashore, looked it over and hailed the other canoes as they rounded the bend.

What a wild and lovely spot! The clouds were breaking up and through a rift we could see the promise of a good day tomorrow. Ducks were constantly in the air for this was a flyway between their feeding grounds. The river gurgled past the ledge, and below us were the rapids we would have to shoot in the morning. There was plenty of room for tents. The fire would be on a flat shelf close enough to the water so I could dip up what I needed without having to make a trip to the river's edge.

There was a good supply of dead spruce and jack pine and much of it was dry, in spite of the rain. In a short time we had a fire going and the tents up. Omond was at his usual ritual of concocting a potion suitable for voyageurs who had braved a storm, met Father Moraud, and come through another rapids. His mixture of rum and hot lemonade took the chill out of our bones and made us forget the long dreary stretches in the rain. There was only one toast that night:

"To Father Moraud."

Tony the fisherman made a few exploratory casts along the rock and almost every effort brought a strike. In just a few minutes there were plenty of walleyes for dinner and break-fast. Swiftly I filleted six of them, and because we were white men without the Crees' taboos about frying, dropped them in the pan and let them brown. The clouds had disappeared, and the sunset was wild and beautiful. Eric was again in fine fettle, had suffered nothing, in spite of his temperature of the day before. We had run more fast water without touching the rocks, were again on schedule and well on our way in spite of our reprieve on Dipper and the bad weather.

After dinner we looked at the white water below us. It extended way down the river and the horses looked fierce and unmanageable. The center was impossible, but just across there seemed to be a smooth slick close to the bank with one sharply pointed shelf around which the water swirled and spouted. If the canoes could get past that point, they would be all right, but in avoiding it they might be drawn into the heavy waves at the center.

As we lay in our bags that night, we listened to the gurgle of water beside the tents and to the soft steady roar from down below.

"It has been a good day, Bourgeois," said Tony. "Every day is a good day and weren't we lucky about that canoe. How do you suppose it could have been blown off that rock with none of us hearing it and then landing over in those willows without a scratch? The waves going over were pretty big and you didn't see the time we had getting away from the cliff."

Before I could answer, he was breathing deeply with the rushing of the river.

"Come and stay with me tonight." That courtly bow, the brave cassocked figure bouncing up and down on the waves. Some day I'd come back and visit Father Moraud. That was something to dream about.

FROM

OPEN HORIZONS

Unless we keep the stream of the past
with living significance for the present,
we not only have no past but we have no present.
Tradition is not a barren pride in a dead glory;
tradition is something that provides
refreshment for the spirit.

It is something that gives us deep assurance
and a sense of destiny and a determination to
hold fast to the great things that have been done
through valor and imagination by those who
have gone before us.

FELIX FRANKFURTER

CHAPTER IV

STREAM OF THE PAST

THERE IS no better way to re-capture the spirit of an era than to follow old trails, gathering from the earth itself the feelings and challenges of those who trod them long ago. The landscape and way of life may be changed, but the same winds blow on waterways, plains, and mountains, the rains, snows, and the sun beat down, the miles are just as long.

When I first saw the wilderness lake country, I knew little of its past beyond the fact the logging was about over, the great booms, rafts, and enormous mills gone. Old lumberjacks were still around with their stagged high-water pants and the swagger that belonged to them alone. To me that period seemed part of the time in which I lived.

Even the Indians were not entirely of the past, for some still stopped at the old campsites, fishing and traveling the lakes and rivers. Their social system and spiritual beliefs were changing, reservations had been established, areas they used to roam limited. I did not associate this with any different way of life than my own.

Absorbed in the present and involved with my own activities, I simply accepted things as they were. As a boy I had been familiar with the heroes of pioneer days, but this was a legendary period, and there was an unreality about it that had nothing to do with the present. And so it was with the meager accounts I had learned in my American-history studies of the fur trade and early settlement along the St. Lawrence River in Quebec, names like Champlain, Cartier, Radisson, and Groseilliers, and the spread of exploration toward the west were also legendary.

During my guiding in the regions the French voyageurs had traveled, I became friends with some of the halfbreed descendants of these men, and it was they who gave me my first living picture of the past. Joe Bouchard, Leo and Henry Chosa, Pierre La Ronge, and others told stories they had heard as boys of great birchbark canoes that came down the border from far-off Montreal, leaving such names to lakes, portages, and rivers as Lac la Croix, Trois-Rivières, and

Maligne. Until then I had taken French names as a matter of course, but now they began to mean something.

I read Solon Buck's account of the fur trade, and of Grand Portage, the great carrying place on Lake Superior where thousands of Indians, voyageurs, and traders gathered each summer to exchange axes, knives, and muskets for the priceless pelts of beaver—the most famous rendezvous on the continent, the halfway point of a canoe route 3,500 miles in length where brigades from Montreal met those from Fort Chipewyan, and until the early nineteenth century the most vital funnel in the trade and exploration of the northwest. From this isolated wilderness encampment, well known in the courts and banking houses of Europe, expeditions sallied forth to Rainy Lake and Lake Winnipeg, and by way of the Saskatchewan and Churchill rivers to Fort Chipewyan at the far west end of Lake Athabasca.

Grand Portage was one of the longest and most rugged portages of the entire route, nine miles of hills and swamps around the boiling rapids of the Pigeon River, a trail that tested the strength and endurance of generations of French voyageurs. Alexander Mackenzie of the Northwest Company, famed for his discoveries, described them.

"When they arrived at Grand Portage each of them has to carry eight packages of such goods and provisions as are necessary in the interior country. This is a labor which cattle cannot conveniently perform in summer as both horses and oxen were tried by the company without success.

"I have known some of them to set off with two packages of ninety pounds each and return with two others of the same weight in the course of six hours, being a distance of eighteen miles over hills and mountains." He might have added that some even carried three.

Later I read Grace Lee Nute's *The Voyageur's Highway*, as well as the diaries of such explorers as Mackenzie, Vérendrye, and Thompson, and through them caught at last the flavor, romance, and danger of the days in which they lived. The great highway of lakes, rivers, and forests became alive, and when I paddled down waterways, ran the rapids, and made the portages those old canoemen trod, mine was a sense of personal identification so powerful at times it seemed as though I were one of them.

Their story of the two hundred years between 1650 and 1850 was a dramatic one in which fortunes in furs and supplies moved up and down the great highway. It was a time of struggle, warfare, and piracy between the rival fur companies of England, France, and the United States. A vast network of forts and posts was established throughout the north and west, and as a result, the lands were opened up, bringing settlers and development in their wake.

All this was fascinating, but it was the voyageur who captured my imagination, he who carried the tremendous loads, paddled from dawn to dark fighting waves and storms, existing on a diet of pea soup and a daily spoonful of fat. His muscle and brawn supplied the power for all the exploration and trade, but in spite of the harshness of his life, the privation, suffering, and constant threat of death by exposure, drowning, and Indian attack, he developed a nonchalance and joy in the wilderness that has never been equaled in man's conquest and exploitation of any new land. These gay French Canadian canoemen with red sashes and caps, singing in the face of monotony and disaster, were the ones who stood out.

Their contracts with the various fur companies prove profit had little to do with their choice, that it must have been something else, the lure, perhaps, of far places, the romance and adventure of a way of life they had never known before. Whatever the reason, they practically deserted the villages along the St. Lawrence for the pays d'en haute. Before embarking on any expedition, each signed an agreement, usually with a cross, for few could read or write. One to three years was the normal term of service, a bowman or steersman receiving 1,200 livres per annum, an ordinary paddler 400, and for this princely sum he agreed to do whatever was required, not to desert his master or give aid and encouragement to his rivals. A third of the wages was supplied before starting, together with his equipment, consisting of a blanket, shirt, pair of trousers, two handkerchiefs, and several pounds of twist tobacco. The penalty for desertion or insubordination enroute was flogging, or far worse, abandonment in the bush. But in spite of long absences from family and friends, grueling work on lakes and portages, they fought for the chance to go and were proud when chosen for the brigades. No worse fate could befall a young man than to be forced to remain at home.

For several years I guided with a young French Canadian, Pierre La Ronge, in whose veins ran the blood of a long line of voyageurs. From the very first he called me François, and no sooner were we together than we spoke in the patois of Old Quebec from where his people came. The longer this went on the more we acted and felt like the men from Montreal and Trois-Rivières, and after a while we felt more like voyageurs than guides of the twentieth century.

"Pierre," I might say, "when you go for catch dose trout, use hangerworm or hoppergrass."

"*Oui, oui,* François," he would reply in mock desperation, "dere ees no hangerworm or hoppergrass een dees countree. All we have eese copper spoon," and with a gesture of utter bafflement any Quebecer might envy, "What can poor Pierre do?"

When cooking the inevitable dried fruit he would announce to an invisible audience, "De prune ees de fines' berry dat grows een de swamp."

A ridiculous performance, perhaps, but it provided many laughs, and talking like men from the villages along the St. Lawrence somehow colored our attitude toward the life we were leading and gave all events, including the weather, a humorous twist.

If someone should happen to balk at the weight of a pack, invariably he would be reminded of the standard load for voyageurs, the regular 180 pounds of the two packets he had to carry, and of the great La Bonga who put them all to shame with five, a total of 450 pounds. The carrying then was done with a tumpline, a broad leather strap over the top of the head. In those early days of guiding before I had seen the kind of carrying still done by Indians and half-breeds back in the bush, I used to wonder if the old stories were true. Now I know they were, for I have seen what they can do where carrying loads is an accepted thing.

A few years ago during a packing contest, a Cree Indian carried 500 pounds. When I told of this record to some Swampy Crees in the Hudson Bay country to the east, one of them said, "I can carry that too, and the Indian on top," and having watched him on the portages, I believed him.

The Sherpas of the Himalayas think nothing of such feats. Anthony Lovink, a companion of many Canadian expeditions, after years in this part of the world, observed: "They begin carrying as children, gradually with heavier and heavier loads, learning the art of balance, breathing, and conditioning muscles and nerves to cope with the ruggedness and rarefied atmosphere of the high mountains."

And so it must have been with the voyageurs who entered the service young. They learned by doing, and glorying in their strength, portages were a relief from paddling, a place for visiting and feeling the ground under their feet after the hazard of rapids and the waves of big lakes.

Pierre and I were no different, and when after a long paddle we finally hit the shore, we tore into the packs as though each was a personal challenge. Sometimes when the weather was foul and the trails a soggy mess, Pierre would quote from William Henry Drummond, the bard of the fur trade.

"De win' she blow on Lac St. Claire,
She blow den blow some more,
    Eef you don't drown on dees beeg lac
    You better kip close to shore."

But the poem he loved best of all was "The Voyageur." He knew all the verses and sometimes at night when all the work was done and the time had come to crawl into our blankets, he would load up his blackened pipe, light it with a coal, get to his feet, and begin. All would go well until he came to the last verse; then his eyes grew round and dark and his voice husky as he declaimed:

"So dat's de reason I drink tonight
To de men of de Grand Nor'Wes',
    For hees heart was young, an' hees heart was light
    So long as he's leevin' dere—
        I'm proud of de sam' blood in my vein,
        I'm a son of de Nort' Win' wance again—
            So we'll fill her up till de bottle's drain,
            An' drink to de Voyageur."

But the gaudy brigades are gone now, no longer are red-tipped paddles flashing in the sun, no more the singing and the sound of voices across the water, nothing left but crumbling forts, old foundations, and the names they left behind them. But there is something that will never be lost, the voyageur as a symbol of a way of life, the gay spirit with which he faced enormous odds, and a love of the wilderness few frontiersmen ever knew.

This is what Pierre and I thought of when we talked our broken English, and when we were together, ghosts of those days stalked the portages and phantom canoes moved down the lakes. On quiet nights it seemed we could hear the old *chansons* drifting across the water and hear their banter. I know when their story is weighed on the scales of history, the Pierres, Baptistes, and Jeans will be remembered not so much for what they did in the opening up of the continent, but for what they were. Theirs was a heritage of courage and spirit men will never forget.

Having seen most of the country within a radius of a few hundred miles of Ely, I longed to explore to the north and northwest as some of the older guides had done. Recalling their stories of the Albany, Sioux Lookout, and the Flin Flon, I knew the beautiful lake country of the Quetico-Superior was only a small part of the great route followed in the past. As years went by, it became an obsession to know the tremendous distances beyond, and to understand what motivated the voyageurs and the challenges that were theirs.

Though the country was mapped, with long-established Hudson's Bay posts scattered across it, the physical terrain was the same, with vast reaches as primitive as in the days of old.

Thus began a series of expeditions with friends who felt as I. The famous Churchill River was the first, a thousand miles or more of lakes, rapids, and waterfalls extending from Ile-à-la Crosse in Saskatchewan to Hudson Bay. Though I had known the southern fringes of the Canadian Shield, I did not realize its real meaning and continental extent. We ran all the white water we could, lined where we dared not run, fought storms on the big lakes, and came to know the bush I had dreamed about so long.

Once we followed the Camsell River north of the three-hundred-mile sweep of Great Slave Lake from the divide as far as Great Bear, with its cold, desolate barrens southwest of Coronation Gulf on the Arctic Coast. From the west end we careened down the Bear River to the Mackenzie ninety miles away, and for the first time saw the route the famous explorer had followed in his search for the Northwest Passage, only to find its mouth in the ice floes of the Arctic Ocean.

We retraced the trail of David Thompson, beginning at Reindeer Lake, 160 miles to the mouth of the Swan, and finally went down the Fond du Lac to the Hudson's Bay post at Stony Rapids on Lake Athabasca, almost 300 miles from Fort Chipewyan at its far west end. This was the starting place of the famed Athabasca brigades who each year met those from Montreal at Grand Portage some 2,000 miles away.

I saw the caribou migration on the Wolverine-Neganilini country northwest of Fort Churchill, came to know the open tundras beyond the limit of trees, and the feel of the lonely barrens along the west coast of the Bay. Like the caribou, I sought shelter in the islands of dwarf spruce known as the Taiga, the parklike stretches lying between the tundras and the treeline to the south. The land of little sticks, as it is called, Taiga is a refuge for all living things, a sanctuary from blizzards or swirling whiteness, the long night, and the eternal cold.

In 1964 we followed the Nelson, the Esquamish, and the Hayes down the historic route to Old York Factory on Hudson Bay, gazed as countless voyageurs had done over the blue and sparkling reaches of the sea itself, saw polar bears with their cubs, schools of white whales, and felt the frigid blasts from the ice pack in the straits above.

Two years later we saw the Ottawa, the Mattawa, and the French, the beginning of the route from Montreal, heard the legends of Champlain and saw the portage where he lost his precious astrolabe in 1615. We portaged dangerous rapids on the French which had claimed the lives of many voyageurs, pictured the banks with their white crosses where in the high water of spring the great canoes were all but torn apart.

We passed through the narrow dalles all diarists wrote about with fear and delight, the places where parallel, rocky ridges make narrow canal-like chutes through which the canoes speed during times of flood. We did not run them, for this was fall and the waters were low, but as we portaged beside them, we could almost hear the wild shouts as the thirty-five-foot Montreal canoes shot through, the banks close enough to touch. Then in the calm, placid area below, we looked as they had done at the broad, blue expanses of Lake Huron, with its hundreds of rocky, windswept islands and their tattered pines.

I saw the clear green headwaters of the Yukon where it flows from the height of land above Skagway down through the fabled gold fields of 1898, and its brown and sluggish flow as it passes Fort Yukon on its way to the Bering Sea.

I came to know the part the Mississippi, the Missouri, and the Yellowstone played during the fur trade, for they were also highways of the voyageurs into such rendezvous as Jackson Hole in Wyoming. There were no rivers the traders failed to explore, no matter how far or remote. Some ventured so far they never did return, but wherever they went, the goods went with them, packs that grew more valuable with every added mile from St. Louis and Montreal. The rapids cost lives, goods, and fur; every turbulent stretch of white water took its toll.

The explorers and traders spoke with dread of these disasters, the loss of men, valuable canoes and cargoes, but still they paddled on into the beaver country, penetrating farther and farther into the last unsettled lands of the continent.

Charles Grant, a Nor'wester, wrote the governor of Quebec in 1780 that "Indian trade by every communication is carried on at great expense, labour, and risk of both men and property; every year furnishes instances of the loss of men and goods by accident."

According to the Colonial Office Papers of 1786, "67 licenses were granted that year covering 163 canoes, 163 flat bottomed wooden bateaux, 2,130 men, 56,324 gallons of rum, 66,207 pounds of powder, 899½ hundred weight of ball and shot. In addition were the usual packets of ironware, kettles, beads, calico and trinkets gone up river."

Alexander Henry recorded the cargo of a typical canoe headed for the Red River country on July 20, 1800.

Merchandise 90 pounds each	— 5 bales
Canal tobacco	— 1 bale
Kettles	— 1 bale
Guns	— 1 case
Iron works	— 1 case
New twist tobacco	— 2 rolls
Leaden balls	— 2 bags
Leaden shot	— 1 bag
Sugar	— 1 keg
1 case gun powder	— 2 kegs
High wine, distilled, 9 gallons each	—10 kegs

Equipage for the voyage: Provisions for every four men to Red River, 4 bags corn, 1½ bushels in each, private property belonging to the men consisting of clothing, tobacco, etc. for themselves and families for the year, so that when all hands were embarked the canoes sunk to the gunnel.

With such factual knowledge contributed by many explorers and traders, and pieces of equipment found on portages and campsites over the years, historians became convinced that beneath many of the rapids along the Voyageur's Highway was a treasure trove of artifacts, and if it was explored with modern diving gear, they might find some of the places where accidents had occurred.

The Minnesota Historical Society, long interested in the voyageur story, organized a diving expedition to explore the Basswood River between Basswood and Crooked Lake on the Minnesota-Ontario border. This dangerous six-mile stretch had been mentioned by many early travelers and would, without question, be a good place to start.

Knowing voyageurs, like all canoemen, would run fast water wherever they could to save labor and time spent in portaging, we also knew that with their lighthearted approach to danger during the two centuries they traversed this route they must have tried many places where they should have carried, or perhaps after some regale at one of the trading posts they had thrown caution to the winds.

The first diving was done below several of the big, brawling rapids that literally boil around rocks and hidden ledges, where certain destruction would await any canoe coming down. To our surprise we found nothing, but knowing that modern canoemen never attempt such places, run only the easy ones, and that all, irrespective of the age in which they lived, are much the same, we decided after many fruitless and dangerous dives to try the relatively smooth, easy slicks of fast water instead. Even such rapids have whirlpools, treacherous currents, and hidden rocks that can mean disaster when the light is bad, the water too low, or the bow-man a trifle reckless.

We concentrated on rapids they might chance, and it was then the divers found what we were looking for. I shall never forget the thrill of seeing the first emerge with a hand-ful of rusted spear points. We ran to the shore, helped him out of the water, and took the precious iron from his hands.

"There's a lot of stuff down there," he blurted. "More where these came from."

Barely waiting to get his breath, he dove again and was joined by two others, and from then on it was a procession of trips from the bottom of the hole they had found to the shore. Soon there were piles of trade axes, spears, and leaden shot, even beads and vermilion paint, bits of broken pipes, plates, flint, steel, and copper pots.

It could well have been the disaster Alexander Henry the Younger wrote about 165 years before. In a notation of August 9, 1800, he described a typical mishap. "I perceived the canoe on the north side coming off to sault [shoot] the rapids. She had not gone many yards when by some mis-management of the foreman, the current bore down her bow full upon the shore against a rock . . . The canoe we found flat upon the water, broken in many places . . . The loss amounted to five bales of merchandise, two bales new to-bacco, one bale canal tobacco, one bale kettles, one bale balls, one bale shot, one case guns. I was surprised that a keg of sugar drifted down about half a mile below the rapids as its weight was 87 pounds; it proved but little damaged.

The kegs of gun power also floated a great distance but did not leak."

I could imagine a twenty-five-foot North canoe starting down the rapids we were exploring, trying to avoid the big round boulder at its very crest. If the depth of the water was not just right, the canoe could be caught, swing broadside, ricocheting from rock to rock, swiftly filling with water as its great sides of bark and cedar were crushed, its bales sinking into the current, the voyageurs trying desperately to save what they could before scrambling for the shore to save themselves. Then the tragic aftermath, knowing the expedition might well be ended, food, weapons, clothing, blankets, and tobacco gone; ahead, starvation and possibly death.

The divers seemed incongruous in that wild setting with brilliant orange-and-black suits and sky-blue flippers. When they surfaced, coursing smoothly through the water, they were creatures of a different world against a background that had not changed since the days of the trade, the same smooth shelf of granite at the landing, the rounded boulders across the river, the swirl around the big one at the head of the rapids, and the eternal standing waves as fixed and sculptured as though they were carved from stone.

Seeing those artifacts come out of the water where they may have lain for two centuries or more was like meeting the voyageurs themselves. We laid our treasures on the rocks and looked at them with wonder. This is what they had carried and guarded with their lives; those rust-encrusted axes, those knives and spearheads had been handled last by them.

It was not until I stood again on the shore of Lake Superior at the site of old Grand Portage that the full significance and meaning came home to me. Now I could see it all—the Quetico-Superior country, Lake of the Woods and Winnipeg, Saskatchewan and the Churchill. They lay before me now—Athabasca and Great Slave, the Mackenzie and Great Bear, the Nelson and the Hayes, the St. Lawrence, Ottawa and the French, the wide expanses of lakes Huron, Michigan, and Superior, the whole broad sweep of land and water that was theirs. What I saw was a living map of lakes, rivers, and forests, of mountains and plains, a map colored with disaster and disappointment, with challenge and triumph, with hopes and dreams. It took many years to understand the voyageurs and the lives they led; seemed ages since I had guided with Pierre. I thought of him then and wondered if we would have been equal to the challenges that were theirs. I could hear him bellowing into the wind:

> "I'm proud of de sam' blood in my vein,
> I'm a son of de Nort' Win' wance again—
> So we'll fill her up till de bottle's drain
> An' drink to de Voyageur."

When I saw the name Samuel Hearne chiseled in the rock off Fort Churchill on the west coast of Hudson Bay with the date 1789 below, it meant more to me having seen the Coppermine and the Arctic Coast he finally reached.

I never see the Mackenzie River without sensing the

heartbreak of the great Alexander when his dream of finding the Northwest Passage to the Orient came to naught, when after thousands of miles of travel, he found it was only another way to the Polar Sea. I can picture him looking across the endless ice floes with their fogs and constant whispering, and understand why he named one of the largest rivers on the continent "River of Disappointment."

In Montreal along the old waterfront where thousands of great canoes once embarked for the west, I think of David Thompson, the best mapmaker of them all, and how, in his old age, he was forced to sell his most precious possession to keep from starving, the theodolite he had almost lost on the Fond du Lac, the instrument which helped map more of the continent than any man had ever done.

At old Grand Portage, I like to climb to the lookout place on top of Mount Rose where Daniel Harmon used to watch the busy scene below of voyageurs packing their loads on the portage trail, the comings and goings and frantic preparations of brigades for the northwest or the east. I never see an Indian dance without thinking of John Flatt, the blind chief of the Grand Portage band, listening to the tom-toms with tears running down his weathered face as he remembered young dancers of his past, the dream dancers who may have known the last of the voyageurs. When young braves lounge around some trading post, I think of the night Chief John Graves of the Red Lake Reservation told me there was always something for them to do in the old days, hunting and fishing expeditions, gathering of wild rice and maple sugar, and the war games with distant tribes, the great feasts when they returned and how coups were rewarded and the pride of the tall young men as they boasted of their exploits.

"Today," he said, "there is nothing for them to do. They drink and get into trouble, and sometimes white men put them in jail because they do not understand. This is sad for my people and for all Indians."

History means emotion and a consciousness of what people felt as they lived in primitive ways, endured hardships, and knew triumphs. Whether it was the period before white men came, the time of the voyageurs, Spanish exploration of the Southwest, the long wagon trains along the Santa Fe or Oregon, the wilderness road of Daniel Boone or the mountain men, it is how they lived, suffered, and laughed, and what their dreams were, that determined the course of history. We can read and study, look at pictures and portrayals of those days, but the real heritage is knowing the land and those who lived upon it.

I followed the Wilderness Road of Daniel Boone across the Smoky Mountains toward the dark and bloody ground of Kentucky. The wilder reaches of those mountains look much the same as they did then, the views from grassy balds of high billowing hills, and the drifting clouds and floating mists which gave them their name. Coming by foot through Cumberland Gap for the first time and breaking out into the open meant more because of the wilderness I had known elsewhere. I could guess better the feelings of the first frontiersmen after days of climbing and hoping each ridge was the last. There in the distant blue was the unknown, hostile Indian tribes with the possibility of capture, torture, and death; I sensed their fierce joy as they thought of the land-hungry people waiting for word it was safe to move on. These men were not voyageurs in a wilderness of lakes and rivers; this was a land of dark forests and broad valleys, a land of twilight and shadows and the eternal sounds of hidden springs and rivulets.

In tracing the sun-baked trail of the Spaniard Coronado as he sought the Seven Cities of Cibola across the arid canyons and painted deserts of the Southwest, I knew what he and his men had experienced, the thirst, blowing sand, and withering heat of a land where there was no shade. From the moment the copper ball of the sun climbed above a blazing horizon until it sank trembling into the blue dusk, there was no relief. Day after day, it was the same slow plodding through hot drifting sands with a mirage before them, the glistening spires of Cibola. This was where the conquistadors faced their unknown.

In following Lewis and Clark on the upper Missouri, I marveled at the strangely sculptured cliffs and pinnacles bordering its headwaters two thousand miles from their starting point at St. Louis. I saw the Shining Mountains as they did after traversing the great plains through which the river wound toward its confluence with the Mississippi. We ran the breaks, as they called the upper rapids, portaged and lined as they had done, passed the Buffalo Jumps where Indians drove herds of the huge animals to their death on the rugged talus slopes below, we knew better than the explorers did the mountains ahead, the canyons, peaks, and passes, between them and their goal, the Pacific.

Once when the dogwood and redbud were in bloom and the ground lush with the first flowers of spring, I hiked with a group led by Justice Douglas down the old towpath trail from Cumberland at the head of the Potomac 189 miles to the tidal basin at Washington, D.C. This was the route of the famous Chesapeake and Ohio Canal built during the 1830's when the rivers were still major highways in the East. That spring I saw the river and its beauty, met its people, and skirted rapids boiling their way toward the sea, surprised a flock of great white swans resting on the waters of a quiet bend. There were tracks of deer and coons, and trees were alive with migrating birds.

We passed General Braddock's Road, built during the French and Indian Wars, crossed the far more ancient war trail of the Iroquois. The Civil War had been fought along the Potomac too, and the battlefields lay near. One day I left the towpath and hiked to Antietam, where thousands had died. It seemed strangely peaceful and unreal, but somehow I felt a little closer to those who had fought there and had seen the same trees, the flowers, the rising mists of morning.

As vital as the historic places are the people who live along the river as they have since colonial days. I visited one evening with an old couple above Fredericksburg. Dusk was settling, whippoorwills were calling, night hawks zooming overhead; no other sounds but the gurgling of water. When it grew opalescent, it seemed the scene had never changed.

"I like living here," said the old man. "Family came before the Revolution. The boys and girls moved to town, but we stayed on, Ma and me. Every so often they come back to visit, sit outside the cabin as we're doin' now, remembering when they was kids. You can still take a catfish in the river and when shad's runnin' it's almost like old times. Sometimes when the moon is full I take the old hound dog and run down a coon."

Just then we heard a baying along the ridges above the bottoms. The old man listened intently.

"That's old Major," he said. "He's on the trail of one right now."

As we sat and visited, talk of war and trouble seemed far away.

"No," he said in answer to my query, "I ain't ever goin' to move. This is where our roots are."

I rose to leave, but he begged me to stay and I followed him inside. He lit an oil lamp, touched a match to the kindling in the fireplace, then over a pitcher of apple cider we looked at an album of pictures taken during the days when the canal was still in use. As a boy he had driven a mule along the towpath, and he told me how, when rival crews from the barges would meet at the taverns along the river, there was drinking and brawling until the wee morning hours.

"I remember those days," he said. "A good time to live," and his eyes shone in the firelight.

On the Kern Plateau just below Mount Whitney in California's southern Sierras, I followed the trail of Joe Walker, the famous mountain man, who for forty years between 1821 and 1861 roamed the Southwest. It was he who discovered Yosemite and the Big Trees, and Walker Pass, the route of "manifest destiny" that led to the Mexican War.

He left his mark everywhere in the beautiful southern Sierras, and from Ardis Walker, a descendant and also a mountain man at heart, I heard the story of those adventurous days, of the rendezvous places where Old Joe met with Indians and voyageurs to exchange trade goods for fur.

As we rested our horses one day on Sherman Pass just above the little town of Kernville, we feasted our eyes on vistas of gnarled and wind-blown pines and rugged expanses to the south. I tried to imagine how it must have seemed to those who saw it first and how they felt as they looked beyond the place where we had stopped. The high country was much the same, though logging roads were creeping closer and closer and plans for its recreational development were being discussed.

"Old Joe," said Ardis, "was one of the best scouts of them all, boasted having led more successful expeditions than anyone else without ever having lost a man to Indians, starvation, or accident. Proud of belonging to his clan, feel the same about these mountains."

This was no idle statement, for Ardis, a graduate engineer, had practiced in the East until he could no longer stand the pace and had returned to his beloved Sierras to live. The blood of the old mountain man could not be denied.

With him I gained more of an understanding of those mountains than ever before, for he loved the Kern and the plateau through which it flows, felt the area should be preserved for all time as a rendezvous for mountain men of the future.

And so it has been wherever I have gone; what I learned in the land of the voyageurs taught me what to look for everywhere, convinced me that history means the warmth of human associations, that while great events may find their place in books and museums, it is the people themselves who really counted. No longer did a country provide only opportunities for fishing, hunting, and camping places. I had found something more important. When one followed the trails of the past, no matter who the legendary figures were, voyageurs, conquistadors, or gold seekers, somehow their feelings came through, and when they did, the land glowed with warmth and light.

The North Country is a siren. Who can resist her
song of intricate and rich counterpoint—
the soaring harmonies of bird melodies against
the accompaniment of lapping waters, roaring
cataracts, the soft, sad overtones of pine boughs.

Those who have ever seen her in her beauty or
listened to her vibrant melodies can never
quite forget her nor lose the urge
to return to her.

GRACE LEE NUTE

CHAPTER V

SONG OF THE NORTH

THE SONG of the North still fills me with the same gladness as when I heard it first. It came not only from the land of the Great Lakes, but from the vast regions beyond the Canadian border. More than terrain, more than woods, lakes, and forests, it had promise and meaning and sang of the freedom and challenge of the wilderness. I seemed drawn in its general direction as naturally as a migrating bird is by unseen lines of force, or a salmon by some invisible power toward the stream where it was spawned. Within me was a constant longing, and when I listened to this song, I understood.

There was hunger not only to live in the north, but to know about it, its physical character, people, and the creatures that lived there. I felt I must be on a first-name basis with flowers and trees, birds, fish, insects, and mammals, even the rocks and lichens of its hills and valleys, must know this country and so completely identify myself with it there would be no question of my belonging. I wanted to feel as other creatures did instinctively, that this terrain was mine, and that any place I chose to go was where I belonged.

Not only did I want to share it with all forms of life, but with anyone who would listen. I recall my childish excitement in telling about the first flowers one spring and my joy when I learned what they were. This was an ever present urge within me just as it is with those who are fiercely attached to a country that means more than anyplace else on earth. Watch Alaskans as they talk about the North Star State when far from home; eyes shine, faces are animated as they picture the mountains, glaciers, and tundras of their magnificent land.

Someone said, "Do not take from any man his song," and when I think of the one I have heard, what it has meant and how it has guided me in whatever I have done, I know this warning is true, for when a song is lost, it is seldom replaced. At least so it has been with me, for over the years it has changed my life and influenced all the major decisions I have made.

During the years at Ashland on the south shore of Lake Superior, I attended high school and spent two years at

Northland College, but there was no real consciousness of the north as a place to live. Those days went by as idyllically as the rest of my boyhood, with studies never too important, and most of my leisure devoted to the woods. Only when it began to dawn that the golden age was over for me and that the time had come to leave home for the university did I realize the awful truth. There was never any doubt about going away eventually, but it had always been in the far and distant future.

My father, a Baptist minister, believed there was no question of what a young man should do with his life; it must be dedicated to the welfare of mankind or tilling the soil, never in mundane pursuits having to do with material things. There were only three choices, the ministry, teaching, or farming, and all others were unessential. Though he never urged his sons to go into one or the other, it was always understood, so it was not strange with such a background that spiritual values were the all-important ones. There was never any guidance as I recall, simply that the broad pattern of our attitudes was so much a part of my thinking, I knew intuitively where it would lead.

We lived as many country minister's families did in those days, with few creature comforts or worries about the future. The missionary barrel once a year, donations from members of the church, and a garden plot seemed to take care of all immediate needs, and if at times necessities were scarce, we knew God in His wisdom would take care of His own. Our homes in northern Wisconsin, wherever they happened to be, were always modest and befitting a man of God, but they were full of books, music, and ideas.

There must have been occasions, however, when father looked askance at the roamings of his second son and his complete absorption with the out-of-doors, but if he had any thoughts or forebodings, he said nothing as long as chores and studies were not neglected. My love of nature did not conflict, and when he read such passages at our evening devotions as "Consider the lilies of the field, how they grow; they toil not, neither do they spin," I was reassured. My feeling for the land, for growing things, the sun, wind, and natural beauty were never at odds with the ideals before us.

Unless some part of each day were spent under open skies I was unhappy. Studies, like chores, were something to be done and done well, but my real life was elsewhere. Memories were not of things learned from books, but of broad montages of Lake Michigan off Sister Bay, the rolling surf, crying seagulls and ships, wild flowers along the road-sides in spring, colors blazing in the fall, and the bluish-whiteness of winter's snow. Inland were the vast, cut-over slashings of the pineries, my trail to the hemlock stand and the little creek where I made my camp. Those last forgotten patches of timber were sacred groves to me, peopled with the spirits of the past. On the shore of Lake Superior lay the open expanses to the northeast, the islands beyond Madeline and the endless sloughs of Bad River and Chequamegon Bay. During those carefree years I became part of the north, and the melody I heard was loud and clear.

I remember the heartbreak when I finally left for the University of Wisconsin. Until that fateful day I had not actually faced the finality of going and had nursed the vain hope that something would intervene. As the train pulled out of the station, I sat mournful and alone looking out the window at the familiar scenes I knew so well, the high wooden trestle over the river, the stands of young pine, aspen, and birch, the clearings with trout streams winding through them, ponds fringed with color, sumac flaming from the railroad embankments. I knew I would be back by Christmas, but that day it seemed forever.

During registration I was confused and uncertain, and for some reason thought only of the Namekagon Valley and the dream of having land of my own. I had never really worried about a career or what to study beyond following the general concepts Father had stressed over the years. It never occurred to me that my absorbing interest in nature might be channeled into some field where it could be used, so without more serious consideration, I enrolled in the school of agriculture, a far cry from what the farm really meant, its romance and beauty, and the feeling of being a pioneer.

Through this initial period, I must have been numb with loneliness and longing, for all I could think of was the woods. Gradually, however, new vistas opened up on field trips taken in soils, botany, and geology. Listening to instructors explaining natural phenomena, rock formations, or vegetational types outside the classroom awakened something within me and I began to see the vague outlines of work I could enjoy. Until then I had not pictured what graduation might bring in its wake, but now it seemed that teaching somewhere in the north and near the woods was the answer.

Intrigued with what these young scientists knew, I was excited to explore with them the mysteries of the out-of-doors, and each time we took to the field, they opened new horizons to me. My knowledge had been one of breadth, color, and feeling, but soon grew in depth as I sensed the reasons and learned the stories of evolution and change.

The gloom lifted as I saw the trail ahead. Advisers talked about the possibilities of county-agent work with the University Extension, but this did not have the appeal of teaching and using observations to illustrate courses. Furthermore, teaching was in the sphere of occupations Father approved. All my woods experience could be woven into the task of interpreting the country, and I would not only learn, but pass on what I found to others. In the background, as always, was the hope of moving north. This was what I chose to do.

Shortly after graduation, I was offered a position to teach agriculture and related sciences in the high school of a small mining town in northeastern Minnesota with the Indian name of Nashwauk. Using a map I discovered it was on the Mesabi Iron Range, completely surrounded by a maze of blue with no roads or settlements beyond. That first look was enough, for those spots of blue were lakes, and the wilderness around them conjured up visions that filled me with anticipation.

No sooner had I arrived than I headed out of town to see

what the country was like, climbed a great, rust-colored mound where the gravel, boulders, and low-grade ore had been piled after the surface stripping to expose the beds of iron underneath. As I worked my way toward the top, the dump glowed with orange and yellow in the last slanting rays of sunlight. Below me was the town, a typical mining camp with little box-shaped houses so close together they seemed to touch. Dominating the rest was the school, a large brown building, and two small white churches. There was a single street, lined with the false fronts of stores and saloons, and all around as far as I could see were the scars of open-pit mining, huge excavations, mountainous stockpiles, and brush-covered hills. To the north was a winding dirt road leading out from the range. It was dusk, and as lights appeared and began twinkling over the mines, a red haze covered the grime and raw ugliness and gave it a certain mysterious beauty. I turned and looked behind me. Come Friday, I knew what I would do.

As the week wore on, all I could think of was my coming trip, and when classes were finally over I took my sleeping bag and a little food and followed the road to its end, then struck cross-country into a jungle of burned and cut-over land until darkness made further progress impossible. I found shelter under the spreading branches of a big white spruce, built a tiny fire, and settled down for the night. This was what I had yearned for and was happier than I had been for a long time.

An owl hooted, and the night was filled with rustlings

and sounds almost forgotten. Then the brush cracked sharply and I rose to one elbow—a deer—a moose—then a voice.

"Hello, young fellow—what do you think you're doing?"

Startled, I jumped to my feet. Before me was a burly figure, the face hard and lined, eyes crinkly at the corners and all smiles.

"I'm Al Kennedy," said the man, extending his hand. "Saw your fire from my trail and thought I'd just drop in."

He sat down and I gave him a cup of tea, and he told me about his cabin on McCarty Lake a couple of miles beyond, and of another farther north on a lake he had named.

"You like the bush," he said, poking my fire, "and there's a lot of it here. Drop in on your way tomorrow and we'll have a visit. You must have missed my trail; it's just over the hill and easier going." And then he was gone beyond the firelight. My first meeting with one of the finest woodsmen in the country. It warmed me having him drop in that way, and I knew he approved my Siwash camp.

In the morning I hit the trail early and within an hour was at Al Kennedy's cabin at the end of McCarty Lake. The coffee pot was on, the griddle smoking hot, and we had sourdoughs, venison ribs, and fried potatoes. He told me about the early days, how he had come with the big logging outfits to take out the pine, and when the miners moved in to dig the ore, he had stayed on with them.

"This is good country," he told me. "Lots of lakes and room enough for a man to stretch himself. If you're hungry there's always meat, ducks, and deer, and sometimes a moose, or fish, and with a little garden like I've got, you can raise enough to last all winter. Got some wild rice, too," he added, and showed me a big sack hanging from a rafter. "Picked it myself, parched it like the Indians do. This is the way to live if you like the woods."

I left him then and spent the rest of the weekend exploring the potholes, beaver flowages, and lakes nearby. I did not know then that this was the southern edge of the Canadian Shield, the enormous formation of igneous and volcanic rock which extends far into the Arctic, its ragged fingers spreading under and over the Mesabi Range, and sometimes bursting through the surface in bold outcrops of granite and greenstone. This country had more lakes and streams than I had ever imagined, wild waters with no roads or shoreline developments, McCarty, Shoal, Kennedy, Crooked, and many with no names at all.

My first field trip was to the Hawkins Mine, a gigantic gash in the earth a quarter mile in length and several hundred feet in depth. I wanted to show my geology class the exposed beds of iron and explain the story of their deposition. The excavation was like a miniature Grand Canyon with the whole story of the geological periods there for the reading. One of the shift bosses watched us with interest, and I asked him if he had ever found any evidence of marine fossils.

"No fossils in this formation," he told us emphatically. "Just iron ore. The sea had nothing to do with iron."

Shortly after that as we examined a thin layer of calcareous deposit between two beds of hematite, we did find fossil remnants of ancient fish, indisputable evidence of the part the seas had played in the concentration of the iron formations being mined. From that moment geology became a living science to my students. I had told them about iron-forming bacteria, and the importance of concentration through leaching. No doubt they believed me, but when they found the fossil fish, there was no longer any question. This they understood and would remember.

During that first fall, I practically deserted the classroom, discovered anew the tremendous value of field observation no matter what the general course work involved. Slides, dissections, and books were vital, but only in reference to the living world; better to know a bird, flower, or a rock in its natural setting than to rely solely on routine identification and description. This kind of teaching had as much to do with awareness and appreciation as the actual accumulation of knowledge. Observations on the ground, I decided, were just as important as laboratory experiments; in fact, they went hand in hand, and one without the other was meaningless to me.

On weekends I moved into the woods with the goal of the cabin on Kennedy Lake, a location which became the base for most of the wandering I did. Built on a rise above the shore, it was low and squat, with broad eaves and two small windows to the south. It had a bunk, barrel stove, table, and pegs for clothing and outfit. Outside was a sawbuck and woodpile from where I could look over the whole expanse of the lake.

It was the first cabin I really knew and gave me a feeling of seclusion and settling into the country. Some ten miles from town, it usually took three hours or more to get there, and after learning the way in, I often arrived after dark. There was always kindling in the stove, and though the temperature was often below zero, in a little while it was cozy and warm. That cabin smelled as it should, the indefinable fragrance of balsam boughs, logs, and oakum, and when the fire roared and the light from the open door of the stove flickered over the walls, I felt like a bushrat a thousand miles back in the sticks.

After supper I would get into my sleeping bag and read by the light of a coal-oil lamp how others felt about the wilderness. I often thought as I lay there of Al Kennedy, for whom the lake was named. Al had killed a man in a drunken brawl one spring when the jacks and river pigs had come to town to spend their rolls. He was convicted and served time, but because there was some doubt as to his guilt, he was pardoned by President Theodore Roosevelt. The tale was a gruesome one, but I was sure he had killed in self-defense, for there was never a gentler soul or one with more genuine love of the woods.

There was a bond between us from the first night he came into my camp under the spruce, a bond that grew stronger and stronger. If London, Seton, or any of the rest had known him as I did, they would have taken him to their hearts. Had they watched him talk to his dog, or during the endless hours when he made friends with the chipmunks, rabbits, and deer around his cabin, they would have seen at once the kind of man he was and the love he bore all creatures.

"If you like the woods," he kept telling me, "you should take a look at the lake country east of the Vermilion Range. You can put a canoe in anywhere there and follow those lakes and rivers up to Hudson Bay or west toward Lake of the Woods and Flin Flon. This is a fine country, but wait until you've been there. Once you've seen it you'll never come back."

There were others with the same stories about the Quetico-Superior. A young mining engineer who had worked at the Pioneer Mine at Ely before coming to the Hawkins said: "You can spend a whole lifetime exploring that tangle of lakes and never see it all. There's more water than land, and the only way to get through it is by canoe, just one string of lakes after another, one chain north of Knife on the Canadian side, This Man's–That Man's, The Other Man's, and No Man's Lake. They must have run out of names—the craziest country I ever saw."

I studied the maps and knew what they said was true, decided that during the summer I would take a canoe trip into that fabulous area to see it for myself. When school was over in June, I started for the lake country a hundred miles to the east, and with three young friends from the Mesabi Range, put our canoes into Fall Lake just beyond the town of Ely.

It was a rugged land, a veritable labyrinth of lakes, rivers, and forests entirely different from that around Nashwauk. Logging and mining country, with only a few small clearings between the ridges, most of it was still wild and undeveloped. To our amazement, the pines grew on rocky ledges without any soil, some so twisted and contorted it was hard to tell what they were. The lakes had granite shores, high cliffs rising straight from the water's edge, and rocky shelves smooth as floors, ready for our tents beneath the pines. It was a hauntingly beautiful land, and from the moment we started paddling, I realized Al Kennedy was right, and I would never return to the Mesabi.

After three weeks of traveling some of the major routes through the border country, I knew I would follow those waterways for the rest of my life, not only in the Quetico-Superior, but far into the Canadian north. So powerful was this reaction, and so convinced was I of the ultimate rightness of my feeling, that I decided to return to school and prepare myself for some work that might make it possible to make my living there. I must have more than a bachelor's degree. Graduate work in geology and biology might open the door to a job with the mines, with survey parties prospecting the back country, or with the new junior college being established at Ely. While I hated the thought of leaving, this was the only way to achieve what I had in mind. My love of the woods was stronger than ever, but there was balance now and direction, knowing I would return.

As my work at the university neared its end, I probed every possibility of employment and finally was offered a post as head of the biology department of Ely Junior College. Thrilled with the prospect of actually going there to teach, I accepted with no question as to duties, course work, or salary, convinced that fate had intervened. As soon as I returned I roamed the area, familiarizing myself with rock formations, ponds, and woods within easy reach. By the time classes commenced, I had found enough possibilities within a mile or two to satisfy all needs for field trips. I did not neglect the larger lakes, and on weekends went as far as I could, gradually got to know all the country within twenty or thirty miles. The longer routes would have to wait, but in time I would know them too.

One sparkling October day I took my botany class to a quaking bog. On one side lay a smooth embankment cradling the glacial pothole as with an arm, on the other a tremendous hill of morainic gravel and sand grown with pines. The embankment, or esker, marked the bed of a river that had run beneath the ice, the bog, where a huge block of it had lain long after the glacier's retreat. When it finally melted, there was a deep hollow, the land around smoothed or filled. Full of water for centuries, ten thousand years later it was covered with a springy mat of moss and heather.

As we walked across the smooth brown surface, it gave alarmingly and trembled beneath us. The pines crowded close around, and along its edges were alder and dwarf birch. In the jungle of grasses we found the runways of meadow mice, and in one place a store of carefully gathered seeds. A flock of pine siskins swooped around us, raiding our find, and then flew off to plant them in many places. Squirrels were busy harvesting cones, digging them down into the duff and mineral soil. The forgotten ones might sprout into seedlings, their roots spreading into the mat to give it firmness for the day when the pothole would be part of the surrounding forest.

We learned about the glacial shaping of the area and the plants and animals which over the years had adapted themselves to the habitat, and learned their ecological impact upon it. But more important, perhaps, was the feeling students got of the area itself and of how it evolved.

That winter I met an old prospector who told me about an abandoned gold mine at the west end of Shagawa Lake. "When I first came up here," he related, "there was a gold strike on and prospectors roaming all over. Couple of young chaps found this vein off the Burntside Trail. Can still see 'em the night they came in and laid those specimens of quartz on the bar of the Last Chance Saloon. They were all excited and so was I, for the stuff looked good.

"Went with them next day and followed the road they'd brushed out to the site—a vein two feet thick and ten to fifteen wide going down at a sharp angle. They'd been work-ing for months staking out their claims and making a stock-pile. You can't miss," he said, "even though it's all grown over. That pile of white quartz looms up like a snowdrift through the woods."

When the snow was nearly gone, I took my geology class out there and followed the old tote road with high hopes, my young prospectors as excited about the possibilities as though they were in on a bonanza. The first mile and a half was rough, with windfalls across the trail and tangles of alder and blackberry briers in the low places, but most of the going was clear. We watched constantly for the gleam of white through the trees, but saw only the dark-green wall of balsam and spruce. Then the trail began to rise and finally climbed over a hard rock ledge. We stopped and examined it—slate, iron formations, some intrusions of granite with a few narrow bands of quartz. I divided the group and spread the boys out on either side of the trail.

Suddenly someone yelled, "The gold mine!" And there it was gleaming ghostly and white through the trees. We ran to the shaft and found a great mound of milky quartz, beauti-ful fractured specimens marked with the cobalt blue of cop-per staining, the corroded gray of silver, even microscopic flecks of gold.

This was the first time any of us had seen a gold mine in the bush, and we pawed over the stockpile, crawled into the shaft, explored the area for hundreds of yards around, found the remains of an old cabin, a rusty stove and boiler, and odds and ends of equipment covered with leaves and grass. We were all prospectors that day, finding the vein of quartz and with pick, shovel, and windlass hauling the precious ore to the surface. Years of heartbreaking work had gone into the venture, possibly a fortune, for the men who had found it half a century before. We felt their excitement at the discovery and sensed their despair when it came to naught.

"The assays were pretty low," the old prospector confided, "too low to warrant development. Can still see those boys when the word came back it was just another hole. They worked the mine a little longer, then drifted off to the outside, dead broke as the day they came in."

As we sat in the spring sunshine gloating over our find and getting the feel of breakup in the north, I told them what I knew, how placer deposits accumulated in the beds of creeks and rivers from the erosion of veins such as the one before us, the heavy gold settling to the bottom and laying the stage for panning. I explained how hard-rock mines meant the crushing and chemical separation of gold from the quartz. The boys listened without a word, studying the precious samples in their hands, but I knew what they were thinking. Here at this old mine of the Vermilion rush, they learned about gold and the hopes and dreams of the men who had listened to its call.

A week later while the creeks were still running full and the lakes turning black and showing open leads of blue, I took my zoology class to Lamb's Creek where it empties into

the north side of Shagawa Lake. I wanted my students to
see suckers and northern pike fighting their way upstream
to a grassy meadow where the bottom was sandy and ready
for the spawning. Below a tiny cataract with a pool at its
base, dozens of fish had gathered waiting for the time to
make an assault. Then, as though at a signal, they swam
swiftly to its head, hurled themselves into the swirling stream
among the rocks. Some would lie in the midst of it gathering
strength for the final surge, and then with a violent effort
try again. Most of them made it, but some floated down,
beaten and scarred by the sharp rocks, to rest in the pool
or drift slowly back to the lake.

I picked up one of the suckers; it was hard and cold as
ice, but the fight was out of it. A mink ran along the bank,
its beady eyes watching. I tossed the fish toward it, and
though the little animal disappeared, I knew it would soon
be back to gorge on the welcome flesh.

Up in the meadow we found great northerns swimming
among tussocks of grass and sedge in water so shallow their
broad backs and dorsal fins stuck out. They had left the
creek and were spawning there, though the water would soon
be gone. Some would be stranded if they waited too long, but
it made little difference, for the prime purpose had been
achieved, and while hundreds of thousands of eggs would be
lost, enough would mature to perpetuate the species.

Spawning in the spring was part of the age-old cycle,
budding shrubs and trees, fiddlehead ferns growing out of
the black muck, mink we had seen, blue mayflowers, golden

marsh marigold, and flaming stems of dogwood, the whole vast complex of the ecological system of which they were a part. The feel of spring was there, surging life, sap running in the maples, blisters of resin breaking on the balsams and running down their trunks.

There were times, however, in spite of the stimulation of field trips, when I revolted against schedules and responsibilities and seriously considered abandoning the classroom and heading for the hinterlands where life was less confining. One of these was when Al Kennedy asked me to go with him to the Flin Flon in Manitoba to join the gold rush there and see the country to the northwest. He had gone the year before and returned with tales of gold, herds of woodland caribou, Cree Indians, and Hudson's Bay posts.

He was convinced we would strike it rich if we got there before the rest of the world heard about it, and he knew a hidden creek where the signs were good. All he wanted, said his carefully scribbled note, was a good bow paddler and a grub stake; the rest of the outfit he had. We would start on the Rainy River, northwest of Lake of the Woods, down the Winnipeg to the big lake, then Saskatchewan and the Sturgeon Weir to the Flin Flon, spend the summer and fall there, build a cabin and come out with a fortune in the spring.

The call was upon me and for weeks I thought of nothing else. Torn between decisions, classes and indoors became intolerable, and as spring approached, I did not know what to do. This was my home country now, and with the combination of academic life, contact with young minds, and the opportunity to roam the wilderness, my future seemed full of promise. How could I leave Elizabeth and our two young sons and the home we had established, leave my friends and co-workers and embark on an expedition for a year or possibly two or three, with no assurance we would find what we were looking for? But when I thought of what it would mean to go off on the great adventure, see the far country I had dreamed about and make a fortune as Al was sure we would, I was tempted.

Then one day as I was paddling up the Kawishiwi River and approaching Dead Man's Portage, the answer came. This would not be my only chance at the Flin Flon, for there were many years ahead. I must not leave my responsibilities, had only begun to know the Quetico-Superior, and just skirted the fringes of experience and knowledge. I wanted to be a good wilderness guide and spend summers in the bush working with the men I had met there, getting the feeling that was theirs. Though I was beginning to unravel the geology of this part of the north, in spite of all my exploring I had barely glimpsed the wealth of its flora and fauna, and I knew little of the earth itself and the complex relationships of life in the area. This wanting to know and to identify myself was an absorbing quest as real and as much a part of the north as the Flin Flon country.

With Al Kennedy there was no choice; he must go while there was time. The following summer he took off with another partner, and that was the last I heard of him for several years. There was no fortune in the gold fields for him, but I knew this made no difference, for he had gone and listened once more to the song of the north he had followed all his life.

We are the music makers
    And we are the makers of dreams . . .
For each age is a dream that is dying
    Or one that is coming to birth . . .

ARTHUR O'SHAUGHNESSY

CHAPTER VI

THE MAKER OF DREAMS

THE STUDY of the earth and its shaping opened up new vistas to me, and when finally I was aware of the intricate relationships of all forms of life in the area, my understanding grew to the point where I felt more at home in the wilderness than ever before. The story of Indians, voyageurs, explorers, and settlers added still more color and warmth, increased by the personal associations of guides and woodsmen and the men I cruised with through the lakes and rivers of the Quetico-Superior.

I found during these years that the discovery of any hitherto unknown facet, or even a new way of looking at things, added enjoyment not only for me, but for those with whom I traveled. I learned their feelings about the wilds, and how hungry they were to explore its physical aspects, and anything about the country that made it more meaningful. Loyalties developed to a way of life that seemed the answer to their needs.

As time went on there was a certain fullness within me, more than mere pleasure or memory, a sort of welling up of powerful emotions that somehow must be used and directed. And so began a groping for a way of satisfying the urge to do something with what I had felt and seen, a medium of expression beyond teaching, not only of students, but of those who had been my companions in the wilderness, some medium, I hoped, that would give life and substance to thoughts and memories, a way of recapturing and sharing again the experiences that were mine. The great sculptor Giacometti once said, in surveying his work and dreams:

"Art is only a means of seeing. It is as though reality was always behind a curtain . . . the great adventure to see each day in the same face something new surge forth."

Had I understood then what he meant, it might have explained many things, but I did not know, for the concept of reality as he used the term was incomprehensible to a mind involved only with the visible world and personal gratification.

Days and nights were filled with unanswered questions and wonderings, with trying to clarify values and give direction to my probing, and I sensed vaguely that perhaps, if I looked deeply enough into the wilderness that had satisfied so many needs, the answers might come. My search was so vital to my peace of mind, it completely engrossed me.

During this time I read avidly, steeped myself in all I could find that even remotely had to do with the north, trying to find the secret, not only how others felt about the wilderness, but some hint that might apply to the quest that was mine. Through many books and diaries, I explored the high country of the Rockies and Sierras, the Gold Rush Trail of '98 in the Yukon and Alaska, the waterways and tundras of the Canadian Shield. It never occurred to me that what I really sought was something beyond these volumes and the adventures they held, an entirely different need, the kind of seeing, perhaps, that Giacometti talked about with an interpretation of the land and an emotional involvement that was more than knowledge or superficial enjoyment.

There was other reading too, Emerson, Rousseau, Walt Whitman, Dostoevski, and minds from the distant past, Plato, Aristotle, Marcus Aurelius, and Euripedes. From them I caught glimmerings of wisdom and a depth of perception, man's relationship to man, to his gods, and to the entire universe. The more I read the more I became aware of the need to find a broader vantage point.

I recall the day when I first read *In Defense of Wilderness*, by Euripedes, and the thrill to know that long ago a man mourned the passing of a scene he loved.

> Will they ever come to me, ever again,
> The long, long dances,
> On through the dark till the dim stars wane?
> Shall I feel the dew on my throat,
> And the stream of wind in my hair:
> Shall our white feet gleam
> in the dim expanses?

One day in late October I was hiking back toward town when something strange happened to me, the first of a series of insights over the years. It was as if the thoughts and questions I had been involved with suddenly fell into focus, and in some unaccountable way had been answered so simply and logically, I wondered why I had not known it long before. I looked forward to these moments, for they not only pointed the way, but gave me courage for the task ahead.

It was a melancholy sort of day, skies leaden, the first snow drifting down, a time of introspection in which my own thoughts should have floated as quietly as the flakes themselves. The ground was frozen, ice in the shallows along the shore of a lake I was skirting, leaves and grasses frothy and brittle on the trail, the surfaces of little pools inlaid with long transparent crystals.

The past summer of guiding had been satisfying; I had met many interesting men and explored the lake country farther than ever before. Work in the college had gone well, and the field trips I loved to take had become more and more meaningful because of new studies and observations. I would have been happy and content had it not been for an ever present uncertainty and incompletion that dogged me constantly, the same old questions and wonderings looming as unfathomable as ever, so unanswerable that particular day they almost blurred the beauty around me.

I stopped to rest. A flock of late bluebills were coasting silently offshore, a tight little cluster of black spots flecked with white against the slate of the water. Fall, with its colored violence, was gone, and it was restful to look at the somberness of the shores, the browns, purples, and mauves of hillsides waiting for the storms of November. The ducks barely moved, seemed to keep their position without effort or plan, but even as I sat there, I thought there must be something more than watching ducks, deer, or wolves on my trips into the bush, surely some reason beyond experience or the accumulation of further knowledge, some aim that would give purpose to what I had seen, learned, and thought about. Somehow I must picture the vision within me in a different way than I had ever tried, express my feelings, and catch the country's moods as well as my own.

But how to do this? To explain what the wilderness meant in all its infinite shades seemed an insurmountable task. Poetry might do it, or music, or the colors of a painting, but words, ordinary words—how could they ever begin to portray the sensations that were mine? As I watched the ducks, it was almost as though I had an intimation of what Archibald MacLeish meant many years later when he said, "Art is a human endeavor and the task of a man is not to discover new worlds, but to discover his own world in terms of human comprehension and beauty."

At that time I did not know MacLeish, but the essence of the same truth came home to me that here, perhaps, was my answer, exactly what I must try to do, discover my particular wilderness world in terms of new understanding, describe and paint it with whatever comprehension was mine.

Suddenly the whole purpose of my roaming was clear to me, the miles of paddling and portaging, the years of listening, watching, and studying. I would capture it all, campsites and vistas down wild waterways, the crashing waves of storms and the roar of rapids, sparkling mornings to the calling of the loons, sunsets and evenings, whitethroats and thrushes making music, nights when the milky way was close enough to touch. I would remember laughter and the good feeling after a long portage, and friendships on the trail.

The little raft of ducks floating out in the open were caught that very instant in a single ray of light, and as the somber brown hills were brushed with it, the glow was around and within me. Then the sun dropped behind a cloud and the hills were dark as before, the ducks black spots against the water.

But for a time, I saw them as they were in the glow, and knew nothing could ever be the same again. Had there been the slightest intimation of the long struggle ahead, the many frustrations, the years of hard work and rigid discipline, I might not have had the courage to even dream. If the answer was writing, then it was a tool and medium I must learn to use. What I did not know was that the way I had in mind would take all the resolve I could muster over a long and difficult time, that the real answer to my question lay at the far end of an open horizon different from the rest.

As I came into the little mining town where I lived, everyone seemed unusually friendly, and the main street with its false fronts gleamed, as the hills had. I stopped for a cup of coffee and the waitress must have noticed my elation.

"What's happened to you?" she said. "Find a gold mine back in them thar hills?"

I laughed. "Yes," I replied, "another bonanza."

"No kidding," she said, bringing me my coffee. "Here, drink this and you'll feel better. You prospectors are all the same."

To go into the travail of my early writing is pointless, for all writers, unless geniuses, have the same experience, years of painstaking effort, the gradual growth of facility through endless practice day after day, the interminable disappointments, and the many false starts. Each writer, however, as he looks back, remembers certain milestones, activities, happenings, or events of significance to him alone, perhaps, but nevertheless of great importance.

One of the first for me was taking notes in the field on what I saw and thought about, descriptions of animals, birds, and the countless things observed on each foray into the wilds; until now I had always relied entirely on memory. This was a new activity, and while at first my scribblings were almost incoherent, in time they became more meaningful; but far more important than the actual wrestling with the mechanics of words and sentences was that the very act of recording made me see things more accurately. The longer I tried to recapture scenes and events, the more I saw. I soon filled many notebooks, stories and articles shaped in my mind, and when I finished something I thought was good, I sent it on to the magazines. The fact that these offerings were all returned did not discourage me. There were times, however, when words and ideas came without effort, and I was conscious of something going on in my mind I had not felt before. Golden moments, because they were rare, it was as though writing generated an energy that tapped new sources of knowledge and awareness.

Another milestone all writers will recognize is the acceptance of a first bit of writing. Whether good or bad, it made little difference; the important thing was that for the first time some editor had looked over my work and decided it was good enough to use. What made this a great event was the long time without any success whatever, a period in which it seemed impossible that such a miracle could ever take place.

I had just returned from a guiding trip and was given a telegram. I tore it open, thinking it was a reservation for another fishing or hunting party, but this proved far more exciting.

"Why not write a Sunday feature on one of your canoe trips," said the editor of the Milwaukee *Journal*, "telling us how you go about it, how you travel, describing the country and the fishing."

This last jaunt with three young men of my own age had been especially satisfying. An exploring expedition, we had threaded our way along creeks and beaver flowages, following old Indian and trapping routes few had ever seen. A glorious adventure, we climbed hills, crossed great valleys, and portaged across almost impassable swamps and ridges. I began writing at once, poured out all my enthusiasm trying to describe the country and how I felt about it. The title was "Wilderness Canoe Trip," a story full of all the clichés, romantic feelings, and unformed convictions any young man might be expected to come up with. I labored for days, wrote and rewrote, finally dropped my masterpiece in the mail just before a new fishing party arrived.

On my return, the feature was waiting, and I stared

with unbelief. There were pictures and a map—the spread covered an entire page, but the greatest impact was seeing my name beneath the title. Never again would it impress me the way it did then. This story belonged to me alone, and that day I walked on air, tried to hide my elation and act as though nothing had happened. As I packed a new outfit, the good feeling in me must have shown through.

"What you so happy about?" asked Frankie. "That's a big outfit you're packin'. Don't kill yourself on them portages."

I laughed but said nothing, and when the group joined me a short time later, we were adventurers heading into the blue.

With this bit of success, I was confident the tide had turned, but years went by with no indication from anyone of the slightest interest. The milestone faded into the distance, but my writing continued, for I seemed driven by an urge that could not accept defeat. I dreamed sometimes of the vision that had come to me long before when there wasn't the slightest question, and wondered if I would ever see my goal as sharply again. Perhaps, I reasoned, the medium I had chosen was wrong, the long struggle merely a postponement of the decision to do something else, but I knew there was no other way, and the course was right. There must be faith and hope. Then the vision came again, as though in answer to my indecision, and the dream was reaffirmed.

This time I had gone duck hunting, my goal the rice beds at the upper end of Low Lake, ten miles north of town.

The mallards were still around, and I was sure the stand of rice at the mouth of the Range River would be alive with them. It was Indian summer, a bluebird sort of a day as we call it in the north, warm and sunny, without a breath of wind; the water was sky-blue, the shores a bank of solid gold.

I rested at the end of the sandy and boulder-strewn portage. In one place it had led over a bed of slippery blue clay that sucked at my boots, and once I stumbled and almost fell with the pack and canoe. It was good to drop my load and breathe evenly once more.

Across the narrow bay a log cabin was tucked into a clump of aspen. My friend, the trapper, was laying in a supply of wood for the winter, and the sound of his ax came over the water. After each splitting, he laid the ax aside, stooped, picked up the pieces, and carefully placed them on the pile.

For some reason the scene seemed staged in a sort of godlike leisure removed from the normal frenetic movements of mankind, as though it were part of some long forgotten ancient rhythm reflecting the calm and timeless beauty of that October day.

The ax descended, and a few seconds later came the chuck, as solid and measured as punctuations between intervals of quiet. Again the deliberate action of stooping and placing the chunks of aspen, birch, and spruce on the ever growing rows beside the cabin.

I remembered something I had read, that leisure is a

form of silence in which one becomes part of all creation, and that true leisure is companionship with the gods. At that moment the old dream returned, and I knew that someday all would be realized. I would be more than a watcher of scenes, part of a golden, timeless world.

I threw my pack into the canoe and paddled across the bay, waved as I passed the cabin, then pointed the bow toward the rice beds. The mallards were gone that day, not a wing or the sound of one anywhere, and it was too early for the northern bluebills, but the time was a happy one for my great question had been answered once more.

When I returned, I went at the writing with a determination that brooked no thought of failure. This time I felt the elusive phantom would materialize, and as though the fates had stepped in, one of my stories was accepted by a national magazine.

For a year or more I deluged the editor with manuscripts, but with no success, and then tried *Trails of the Northwoods*, the predecessor of *Sports Afield*. I happened to know the editor personally, and am sure because of this he bought several hunting and fishing stories, but none with the interpretive slant I eventually hoped to have. Some, however, about animals and birds, held more of the feeling I wanted to convey.

"Papette" was the story of a husky dog with so much wolf blood in her veins she always answered the call of the pack when the mating urge was upon her.

"Snow Wings" was illustrated by Charles Livingston Bull, one of the best wildlife artists of the time. His picture of a white Arctic owl winging its way over a moonlit valley thrilled me as much as seeing the story in print.

Then came "Buck of Tamarack Swamp," an attempt to capture the essence of the frozen north from deer season on through the winter.

There was tremendous satisfaction when the stories came out, for they had something in them that I wanted to say, some hint of what I was striving to express, but most were far from my major goal. Editors wanted action, and whenever I injected the slightest bit of philosophy or personal conviction, it was usually deleted. At first I accepted the editing with good grace, happy to have them take my stories at any price, but as time went on I began to feel as though I had entered a sort of cul-de-sac from which there was no escape, a grinding out of more and more adventure yarns with nothing in them of my own ideas or knowledge of the country. If this, I admitted ruefully, was what I had gone to the woods to find, I still had far to go. What I did not realize was that the constant honing of my perceptions and writing ability, the continual practice in trying to express myself, was laying the background for eventual acceptance in a field I had not even begun to explore.

There was one exception, an article entitled "Search for the Wild," in which I quoted the statement of Thoreau beginning "We need the tonic of wildness," and a criticism by

John Burroughs in which he said, "Thoreau went to nature as an oracle, questioning her as a naturalist and poet and yet there was always a question in his mind . . . a search for something he did not find."

To me this was a challenge, and convinced that the lifetime search of Thoreau had been fruitful and what he sought and found in the woods and fields around Concord, Walden Pond, and the Merrimack River was what we all seek when we go into the bush, I tried to prove that the never ending search for the essence of the wild was the underlying motive of all trips and expeditions.

I had dared speak of my deepest convictions, and for once there were no deletions. The first real encouragement I had ever had, it convinced me there was a field for this kind of writing. But again progress was slow, the milestone forgotten, and the next years no different from those that had gone before.

In trying to explain my feelings about wilderness, the time had not been wasted, for facility improved, and the reading and study never ceased. Occasionally when I did no writing at all, my spirits fell and everything seemed without meaning or purpose. The only cure was to begin again, and I found it made little difference what it happened to be, a story, an article, or even the transcription of field notes; as soon as I started, my spirits soared. So infallible was this reaction and so sound a barometer of my state of mind, I was sure that in spite of other activities or the worthwhileness of anything I wrote, I must keep on.

There were times when I looked at the growing accumulation of writings with dismay, wondering if anything could possibly come from all the effort that had gone into them. Even as I questioned, another milestone was approaching, a more important one than any of those in the past. To try and salvage a small part of this storehouse of events, descriptions of places, reactions, and feelings, I conceived the idea of doing a news column rather than stories or articles for magazines; it would be an outdoor column devoted to the central idea that had dominated my thinking. The more I analyzed what I had done, the clearer it became that this might be the solution, inasmuch as most of my observations inevitably developed into short, interpretive vignettes. I worked up a series of topics such as "Smell of the Morning," "Caribou Creek," and "The Pond," and sent them to the Minneapolis *Star Journal*, where they appeared as Sunday features. Letters came from many readers, and the reaction was always the same; I had put into words how each felt about the out-of-doors.

A Chicago syndicate, on the strength of these, made me an offer to do three columns a week for a number of papers in the Great Lakes area. Following a personal interview and a contract, my mind seethed with ideas and plans and I went home to what seemed a new and exciting era.

All my energies were concentrated now on the preparation of material, and I combed forgotten collections of notes in building a backlog of articles that would keep the venture going for a long time. For a year the column prospered, then one by one the papers began dropping it.

"Not enough action," said the editor. "We want more fishing, hunting, and adventure."

The fledgling column of interpretive vignettes was on its way out, and one day came the long expected letter from the syndicate, and I was back where I began. I looked sadly at the collection of completed columns, and lists of titles for the future, and wondered which way to turn. Maybe after all my dream was an impossible one with no chance of realization.

All was not lost, however, for there were many completed sketches and a good acceptance, in spite of what the editors said. More important, perhaps, was that under pressure to meet weekly deadlines, it was no longer as difficult to recapture scenes or impressions. When the work had gone well, ideas fairly swarmed, and some of the sketches almost wrote themselves. I remembered being so completely absorbed I forgot all else in the joy of actually writing what I wanted to say. While there seemed no hope at that time, I had learned a great deal, and strangely enough my determination was strengthened by the battle to find expression.

A new type of writing began, enlargement of the vignette into more comprehensive essays. With them as a core, there seemed no limit to the possibilities ahead, and I felt that here at last was a field, unlike any writing I had ever done. I forgot the failure of the column and went to work with confidence. One day I wrote:

"I have discovered I am not alone in my listening, that almost everyone is listening for something, that the search for places where the singing may be heard goes on everywhere. It is part of the hunger all of us have for a time when we were closer to nature than we are today. Should we actually hear the singing wilderness, cities and their confusion become places of quiet, speed and turmoil are slowed to the pace of the seasons, and tensions are replaced by calm."

This was what I had always wanted to say, and really believed, the secret that had eluded me so long. Here was the dream. The essays would be brought together in a book, or a series of books, encompassing all I had ever done, thought about, or cherished. Somehow the words would come if I were true, and those who loved the wilderness would remember where they had been. I knew how they felt, had listened to their stories, seen the light in their eyes when they spoke of what they had known.

The following years were crowded with new and challenging activities, including an assignment in Europe with the army and State Department. Upon my return, I resigned my position with Ely Junior College to devote more time to writing and the preservation of wilderness in the Quetico-Superior and elsewhere. While my travels took me all over the continent, somehow the essays grew and matured until there were finally enough for a collection, which I called *The Singing Wilderness.*

One of my happiest days was when the distinguished publishing house of Alfred A. Knopf accepted the manuscript, assigned an editor who felt as I did and who understood what I had tried to say.

The artist, Lee Jaques, an old friend, had promised long before that if I ever wrote a book, he would do the sketches. His beautiful set of black-and-white drawings not only caught the spirit of each essay, but embodied his own powerful gift of portraying the north he loved. With his artistry and Alfred Knopf behind me, nothing could go wrong, and I faced publication with confidence.

Even with this assurance, the publishing date set and the review copies out, I waited with apprehension, well aware of the past and how often editors had shied from my particular approach. There was a good, solid feeling within me, however, for I had done what I had always wanted to do—written as I felt I must.

Then came *Listening Point,* the story of my cabin; *The Lonely Land,* an account of an expedition down the Churchill River in Canada; finally, *Runes of the North,* covering the Quetico-Superior and the entire spectrum of my experience in Canada, the Yukon, and Alaska. I know better now what Giacometti meant when he said any creative activity was a way to reality, seeing something new in the familiar, and the truth so well expressed by MacLeish, that the task of all men is to discover their own world in terms of comprehension and beauty.

Once while traveling between Frankfurt, Germany, and Berlin, a Russian gave me a translation of Kropotkin. Though the war was over, its evidence was all around us, ruined cities, stark concentration camps, and the eyes of hungry impoverished people. There was comfort and stability in Kropotkin, and I searched as I always did for the secret of his great success. Then I found it, and all the horror disappeared and I thought only of what I must do when I returned.

"When the poet," he said, "has found the proper expression for his sense of communion with the cosmos and his fellow men, he becomes capable of inspiring millions."

This had meaning for all who were striving for expression. I might never reach his goal, but when I thought of his "sense of communion with the cosmos" I knew at last my question had been answered, and that this was the goal of my life.

No writer is ever satisfied, but my urge now is to make full use of what I have found and known, to keep blowing upon the coals and ashes of old fires to make them blaze again. This is an open horizon entered long ago, and while headlands, islands, and vistas have shown themselves over the years, as I look ahead there seems to be no end to the mirage of water and sky extending on and on into the distance.

Something lost behind the ranges,
Something hidden, go and find it.
Go and look behind the ranges,
Something lost behind the ranges,
Lost and waiting for you. Go.

KIPLING

CHAPTER VII

BEYOND THE RANGES

WHEN I became a guide in the
Quetico-Superior, I did not realize what it would mean be-

yond satisfying the urge to see new country. True, I had lived close to the woods and relatively unsettled areas most of my life, but there was something that could not be absorbed on short forays limited to weekends or occasional camping trips during the summer. What that early period lacked was the overall cumulative impact of being away for weeks or months at a time. I needed to know what it was like to work in the woods with constant searching for the same down-to-earth authenticity I had found on the homestead in northern Wisconsin. I felt that only by knowing the men who made their living there could I ever really understand and catch the full flavor and meaning of the land itself.

After the guiding season was over, these men worked in the logging camps or in the mines, ran trap lines, or did some outlawing if the price of beaver was right. I would return to the classroom and, like them, dream of the spring breakup when the lakes would open and we could take to the canoe trails again. The fact I came from the outside was against me, I knew, but I was confident I could prove myself and be as resourceful and competent as they.

When I came to Ely, I had two summers of canoe travel behind me, and while this was only a start, I began exploring all the lakes within reach until I felt more at home. Much of the country, especially on the Canadian side of the border, was poorly mapped, and I learned by trial and error how to find my way. All large lakes had connections of some kind with others, sometimes rivers, often little creeks, or in some cases merely seepages through sand and gravel. The secret was to find where the water moved, a matter of studying the horizons to determine their lowest points. Black ash, alder, and muskeg often gave them away, and after a time it became second nature knowing the way to go. There was evidence of portages, indistinct and grown over with brush and blocked by windfalls, but the old trails traveled by Indians for centuries and by prospectors and trappers before me, were there.

I vividly remember my first long trip beyond the border, the sense of unlimited waterways and space, the feeling of being able to travel anywhere if there was enough water to float a canoe. I learned the locations of smooth, glaciated shelves of granite, campsites for which the country is famous, kept in mind vistas of sunsets, moonrises, protection from prevailing winds, discovered such places were few and far between, and that it was well to have them in mind and spaced no more than a day's travel apart.

A good supply of firewood was important, for it was embarrassing to have to look for wood after camp was made. In tree-covered terrain it might seem ridiculous to have to search for fuel, but there are places where everything is green and where there have been no forest fires or blowdown for long periods, or where Indians or others have picked them clean.

Most parties came for the fishing, and I learned that trout thrive in deep, clear water and on rocky bottoms, that in the spring they can be caught off shallow reefs where they have spawned; walleyes need rocky shores and reefs, but not the extreme depths of trout; great northerns like weedy bays, bass smaller ponds with dark waters bordered by lily pads and windfalls along the shores. Some of the larger lakes had all four species, each in its own particular environment. All this was stock in trade.

I knew the haunts of moose and deer, nesting places of herons, ospreys and eagles, beaver dams and flowages that connected lakes, the places where mink, otter and muskrat lived. I found the cliffs where Indian pictographs had been painted by ancient tribes, sites of old villages and trading posts, steeped myself with the kind of information I believed my parties would want. My background of woods experience helped, for the land and all its creatures were old friends.

I practiced using all the cooking information I had, made pan bread or bannock, even cakes and pies in a reflector oven, steaked and broiled fish, and made various stews and combinations. There was much to learn, especially from the guides I met, for they had become expert chefs, an entirely different role than satisfying one's own hunger.

These men, it seemed to me, had been everywhere, to the Sioux Lookout country in the north, down the wild, roaring Albany northeast to Hudson Bay, and to the fabulous gold fields of the Flin Flon in faraway Saskatchewan, casually mentioned names that filled me with excitement, the open doors to a vast and unknown world. The more I heard of these places, the more powerful grew my longing, to see not only all the lakes and rivers along the border, but the uncharted regions of the whole Hudson Bay watershed and the Northwest Territories of Canada as far as the Arctic Coast.

I wanted more than the actual guiding; I needed to know these guides and their feelings about the country they had explored, what motivated them and why they lived as they did. They were a breed apart, as distinctive in their way as the cowpunchers or mountain men of the west.

One was Buck Sletton, newly out of the U.S. Marine Corps, big and burly with a wry sense of humor that colored all he did. No trip was serious as far as he was concerned; he made money at poker, badgered his crew unmercifully, made them feel each trip was a hilarious adventure, that loafing and having fun was far more important than scenery or fishing, and that anyone was insane to work if he didn't have to. His trips were always short, the portages easy, his cooking nondescript, but his parties loved him and swore they had never had a better time.

Arne was a little squint-eyed Finn not much more than five-foot-six, weighing about a hundred and forty pounds; though slight of build, he was all wire, nerve, and sinew. To look at him you wouldn't think he could be much good on a portage, but that body could carry a heavy pack and an eighteen-foot canoe, a load weighing close to two hundred pounds, without strain or apparent effort, the only trace a tightening of muscles along his lean jaws. He rarely said much, was efficiency itself, a good cook, and always knew where the best fishing was.

Gunder Graves, a lumberjack who stayed on after the logging, dressed as all the jacks did—highwater pants, a round, black felt hat cocked just so—and had an air about him of all river pigs of those early days. Tall, angular, and ruggedly handsome, he was more at home with a double-bitted ax or a peavey than with a paddle, but had taken to the canoe trails as though he had never done anything else.

Then there were Frankie and Steve Mizera, brothers who often guided together. Of Yugoslavian descent, their families came to work in the iron mines at Ely. Raised close to the wilderness, they moved into it as naturally as their forebears into the mountains of their homeland. They were much in demand, and in their swarthy compactness and love for the woods, they looked like the Frenchmen who had preceded them.

Matt Heikkila, the very first of them I met, was down to meet the train when I came to Ely. I have never forgotten him; the broad-rimmed hat, pants stagged halfway to the knee, high cheekbones and slit eyes, deeply tanned, with a look of power and poise about him—to me he was the epitome of all woodsmen in the north.

A mixture of nationalities, these were not settlers, for there were no homesteads to open up as in the country to the south. Loggers, miners, and trappers when there was no guiding, expert canoemen, resourceful, and with a lusty sense of humor, they were in a class by themselves. As one said, "Anywhere I hang my hat is home to me," an attitude that prevailed with all of them as long as they had an outfit, some grub, and a party to guide. This same sense of being happy anywhere in the bush I have since found in the far north and in Alaska. An old sourdough summed it all up when he said in telling about his travels, "No matter where you go—there you are."

Over the years they had developed a certain woodsman's dress, not consciously, for they had no guile or flair for romanticism. What they wore was proved by time in mining and logging camps from the coast of Maine to the pineries of the great lakes. Boots were the famous Jefferson Drivers with ten-inch tops and hobnailed soles that made their mark on the river drives, pants usually of heavy duck, fringed and stagged halfway to the knee, a broad belt with a sheath knife, a checked woolen shirt, and a weatherbeaten hat. For bad weather there was always a plaid jumper, but no fancy rain shirts, tightly woven windbreakers or anything resembling modern gear. Their personal outfits were as simple. Guides had no tents for themselves, slept under the canoes, were seldom supplied with sleeping bags, tarps, or mattresses. Such things were for city men, not for men of the bush.

These were the men I wanted to know and work with. Though they put on a show of guiding solely for the wages involved, within each was a deep need that kept them on the trails year after year. Counting the days until they could head back to town, once there, with a drink or two under their belts, a meal someone else had cooked, and a night's sleep in a bed, it soon palled, and they were ready to head back once more.

I met Arne once after a three-month trip toward Sioux Lookout and Lake St. Joe. He came in ragged, hard, and loaded for bear, laughed as he unpacked his outfit and stowed it away. "I've had all the bush I want for a while," he told me. "I'm going to take it easy and sit for a spell."

The very next day he confided almost sheepishly he had an old party going out. "I didn't want to go," he said, "but you just can't turn 'em down," and as he worked away at a new grub list, he whistled softly to himself. And so it was with the rest; the only griping was when they had to wait too long between trips.

Half a century ago the Quetico-Superior was a man's country, with women and children and family groups never straying far beyond the little vacation resorts near town. All parties hired guides, for the interior maps were sketchy at best with blank spaces no one had ever bothered to fill in, and it was a common boast that to the north, outside the thin lines of steel of the Canadian railroads, there wasn't a town or road as far as the north pole.

Beyond the Quetico was a vast lake region of black spruce bogs, with birch, aspen, and balsam on the highlands and scattered stands of pine. This was moose country, and until the turn of the century, woodland caribou. Great gray timber wolves, marten, fisher, and beaver were everywhere in this labyrinth of waterways, rugged canyons, and boulder-strewn valleys. It was a beautiful land with a fatal charm for all who knew it.

This was the wilderness canoe country, and because the guides were the only ones really familiar with it, they met their parties nonchalantly, sure there would be no arguments about routes or procedure. Theirs was complete assurance, and men coming in for trips sensed it, accepting immediately and without question decisions as to what to take or leave behind. To discard some precious item that had been chosen with care and much expense for this special expedition was often a heartbreaking experience.

I can see Buck looking disdainfully at an extra pair of new boots and, without saying a word, tossing them into the discard pile. "If you want to pack 'em over the portages," he would say, "it's your funeral."

That first spring at Ely when I was hoping to get a guiding job with Wilderness Outfitters, I watched the guides getting ready, and marveled at the ease with which they whipped unwieldy mounds of food and equipment into convenient loads for canoe travel. First the empty packs were laid out with a blanket or two in back for cushioning. The cooking outfit went into one, the bag with the nesting pails, the one for knives, forks, and spoons, another for the frying pans, with plates, dishups, pot covers, and cups nestling snugly inside them, the ax with its leather sheath tucked into one corner, the reflector oven always against the back. The tent would go into the pack with the tarps, neatly folded or rolled. Each man had his own personal pack and woe to him if he had more than it could hold. This taught him more about what he could take along than any amount of ribbing, for it was his, and anything extra, tackle boxes or rods, he carried in his hands. The food took up most of the weight in the bottom of each precious pack, and safely against a blanket went the canned goods, and on top, the softer rations, sugar, flour, rice, and beans. Slabs of bacon made good back rests, took the curse off sharp-cornered tins and bits of equipment.

It seldom took a guide more than an hour or two to get his outfit ready, and when he was through, everything was neatly piled and tagged. The pack was known as the Duluth, developed during the days of logging and prospecting in the lake states; easy to throw into a canoe and easy to take out, it was ideal for this type of travel, and on the portages with the leather tumpline as a concession to the voyageurs of old, it never needed improvement.

Most of the guides, I found out, knew only a few major routes when they began, relying on their intuitive knowledge of where the rivers ran as they went along. During the two summers I had traveled the lake country, I learned as they, by dint of much sloshing through bogs, climbing hills and trees, and cutting trails through the woods. This was more important in those days than having maps, for in areas where there seemed to be as much water as land, you could paddle almost anywhere and be sure of coming out in the general direction you chose to go. To be sure, they did get lost once in a while, but not for long, for within each of them was a panorama of the country and a general understanding of the terrain that made confusion temporary. It gave me confidence for the time when I would be heading out on my own.

I waited around the outfitting station for a month, hoping the guides might need an extra man, or some party blow in without a reservation, but day after day it was the same, the old ones already spoken for, and though there were only fifteen, there were always enough to go around.

The day finally arrived, and I'll never forget it, the 23rd of June, 1923, almost two months after the lakes had opened up and were free of ice. The whole crew happened to be out when that fateful wire came announcing the arrival of two men on the noon train. I can see Pete and Joe, managers of the outfit, staring hopelessly at the scrap of yellow paper.

"Guess you're it," said Pete with resignation. "You'll have to take care of 'em, two men, ten days, three hours to pack."

I worked madly throwing the outfit together, laid out the packs, put in the blankets, the cooking outfit, the tent, made out a grub list, checked and double-checked every last item, rolled the glassware, jam, ketchup, and pickles in cardboard strips to prevent breakage, stowed everything away ready for travel, checked an eighteen-foot guide's model Old Town canoe, fitted in a yoke, tested the paddles, found marine glue for patching, put an edge on the ax, saw to buckles and straps, repaired a torn bit of canvas, buzzed around like a squirrel storing cones in the fall, and met the train on time.

At precisely one thirty P.M. it came around the bend as always, but this time whistling and wheezing through the rock cut as though the engineer knew the importance of his cargo. I would take them along the border west to Saganaga, down the Saganagons River to Kawnipi and south through the Agnes-Louisa chain, about a hundred miles all told.

The engine roared into the little station, ground to a screeching halt in a cloud of steam and smoke. The conductor swung off the steps of the lone passenger car and grandly set down the stool.

I tried to appear as nonchalant as the old-timers, hoping no one would guess the wild excitement within me. At the very last two men stepped down, dressed neatly in khaki and high boots; each had a bundle of casting and fly rods. The instant I saw them, I knew it meant a different route.

"All I want is some good bass fishing," said Dave Nelson, the older of the two. "Roger feels the same way, and if we can hit some little bass lakes, that's all we want."

I remembered a lake Walt Hurn, the Canadian Ranger, had told me about east of Crooked, a lake no one fished. We would not go to Saganaga, but down the Basswood

River instead, into Crooked, and head north. Walt could tell me exactly how to find it, and if it was good, we'd camp there the whole time and try some of the other lakes nearby.

We got off in the usual flurry of confusion with not a word from anyone that this was my maiden trip. By the time we reached the first portage seven miles from the landing at the end of Fall Lake, Dave and Roger had begun to settle down. Somehow the packs found their way across, clumsily, perhaps, but with laughter and groans and shouts of encouragement. Neither had ever made a portage before, but when I showed them how to throw a pack by balancing it on one thigh, and with an arm through a shoulder strap swing it into place, they caught on quickly. On Newton Lake I could see them begin to work into the rhythm of paddling, and by the time we reached the last portage of the day at Pipestone Falls, they were acting almost like veterans.

Our first camp was on a bare, rocky point in the full blaze of the sunset. I started the fire, put on the pots of water, helped Dave and Roger put up their tent, showed them how to make a bough bed and lay out their blankets, and left them fussing with their tackle.

"When you're through," I told them, as I went back to my fire, "try for some walleyes off the rocks."

While I cooked potatoes and dried fruit and made a pot of tea, they broke out the casting rods. Dave had one immediately and brought it in. Roger followed with another, and before the potatoes were done, had three, enough for supper and to spare. They watched with great interest as I cut around the gills, sliced along the backbone, removing the skin from the steak held flat against the blade of a paddle, and presto, had six glistening fillets all but quivering they were so fresh. I washed them, sprinkled the strips with flour, laid them in the frying pan, and together we saw them change to golden brown.

It was dusk by then, the loons beginning to call, and below us we could hear the rush of Pipestone Falls, and far to the north the deeper thunder of Basswood. They gorged themselves, sat around awhile, then went to their tents and soon were fast asleep.

I learned then that the work of a guide is never done; in spite of weariness, it is his job to do the chores and be ready for an early start in the morning. I did the dishes, picked out what I needed for breakfast—bacon, coffee, cereal —opened a can of condensed milk, and covered the food packs in case of rain. I put a few boughs under the canoe, strung my mosquito bar from the thwarts, tucked some birch-bark and dried spruce twigs into the bow where it would stay dry, finally checked the tent ropes, and only then turned in.

The morning was bright and we were under way by seven. Rocky islands sparkled in the sunlight, the breeze was at our backs, and the loons were laughing gaily. We were heading for the Canadian Ranger station at King's Point fifteen miles away to pick up licenses, and visit with Walt Hurn before going down the river to Crooked. Shortly before noon, we saw the tall pines of the point and the log cabin just behind them; a little closer and we caught the gay flutter of the Union Jack. Walt greeted us warmly, made out fishing permits for Roger and Dave, but of far greater importance, gave me my first Canadian guiding license. I looked at it with respect, the seal of the Province of Ontario across the top, and down in the lower right-hand corner, the date and Walt's carefully scrawled signature.

"To get to the bass lake," he told me, "go down Crooked about ten miles and look for a bay toward the east. No one has been in there, but there's lots of big bass, saw them swimming right next to the portage."

We paddled in the direction of the roar of Upper Basswood Falls, made the first carry around them, and five more before we reached Crooked Lake. I was tempted to run a couple of them, but thought better of it, knowing that if anything happened, the trip would be ruined before it began. By midafternoon we were drifting by the bold cliffs of the Pictured Rocks, looking at the Indian paintings and wondering what they meant. We passed Table Rock, where the Chippewa and Sioux had a meeting after one of their many wars, and near dusk found the portage at the end of a swampy bay. By dark we were across, heading for a rocky island a quarter of a mile from shore. It was not a good campsite, but it was late, so we unloaded, dragged our outfit up to where it was reasonably level, and made out as best we could. After a hurried supper we sat listening to the loons. Bass were jumping down at the shore, and that was all we needed to know.

In the morning we found a beautiful island grown with huge pines and a smooth, rocky shelf for our camp. A deer greeted us and bass swam in the lily pads where we landed. As soon as camp was set up we got into the canoe for our first fishing, Dave using a casting rod with a pork chunk, Roger a fly rod with a bucktail.

Dave cast out, allowed the bait to lie quietly for a moment, then twitched it gently. A bass took it with a tremendous swirl, and when the fish felt the barb, it stood on its tail and danced across the water. While Dave was playing his big one, Roger had another on his fly, and the two played together. Before we were halfway around the island, we had taken six, between two and five pounds apiece.

"This is what we dreamed about," said Dave. "This is what we came for."

And so it was day after day, the bass hitting, the lake all to ourselves. One night, tired of fishing, we went out under a full moon and sang until midnight. We portaged into small lakes nearby, climbed the hills, and picked strawberries on a grassy slope. Before we realized it, the eight days we had allowed were gone. We tore down the tent, packed up, chose a new route for our return, caught some trout in Robinson and Caribou on the way, followed an old outlaw trail toward home. The last portage was a mile in length, but our loads were light and we didn't mind. On a bald surface of rock high above Basswood, we stopped to rest, feasted our eyes on a vista of woods and rocky hills, and in the distance the blue of the lake where we had started our trip.

My first trip completed, come what may, parties would never worry me again. If they were all as happy as this one, guiding would be a joy. In the short space of ten days I had learned many important things, but most of all that friendships ripen swiftly in the wilds.

"We'll be back," they yelled from the platform, and waved until the train went around the bend, and suddenly I felt strangely alone. It was hard to believe that I had never seen them until this trip, and that we had been together only ten days.

Back in the old warehouse, I unpacked my outfit and stowed it away. Buck was in, and Arne too.

"See you brought 'em back alive," cracked Buck. Not a word from Arne, Pete, or Joe, but I had a good feeling inside me, for I knew my first party had been a success.

During those first years I had the good fortune to team up with several of the older men, and while I was usually guide number two, it gave me an insight into how they did things that could have come in no other way. Each one had developed certain skills, the result of many years of living in the woods. None could explain how or when he had acquired them, but whatever its explanation, it worked, and even as I did, they watched each other until inevitably a guide was a broad composite of the total experience of every man he had been with.

Frank Santineau showed me how to make a warming oven by simply filling the biggest pot full of hot water and putting a covered pan on top. Standing close to the fire, here was one that really worked.

Watching Joe Chosa leave the dock one day I discovered something I did not know, that in paddling one must lean slightly forward, swinging from the hips and using the torso so completely there is actually little movement of the arms. All of them, Johnny Peura, Alex, and Johnny Sansted, paddled the same way, and today I can tell an old canoeman as far as I can see him by the easy way he sits in a canoe.

It was Big Bill Wenstrom who taught me how to throw on a canoe. He didn't tell me, but I noticed the ease with which he did it, the balancing on his thighs, the short kick of the hips, the twist of the arms as the canoe went overhead. It took many tries before I could drop one neatly on my shoulders, but when I was finally able to do so, it was the easiest way of all.

Johnny Sansted, one of the finest woodsmen of them all, taught me to use a paper bag for flouring fish, rather than laying out the fillets and sprinkling them as I had always done. A handful of flour in a bag, the fillets dropped in, a few shakes, and they were ready for the pan without any fuss or waste of meal.

Frank Carney told me to drop a pinch of salt into any dried fruit I was cooking to bring out the flavor, and to add raisins or berries to bannock, a truth I knew with bush rats again and again all over the north.

There were countless little tricks of theirs I used, and over the years of my association I developed a vast admiration for their competence and the discipline that governed their actions. While they might seem brash at times and almost reckless in the chances they took, beneath this façade of bravado was a deep respect for the elements and the forces they must face. To be sure, there were tragedies, as there always are when men face storms and rapids and difficult terrain, but these were the exceptions, and when they happened, all of them mourned and took the lesson to heart. There was the time Johnny Pluth drowned on the Basswood River, and Jack Linklater in Jackfish Bay, and Howard Schaefer in a storm crossing the English Channel. They knew all this and remembered, looked at the skies and listened to the rapids with more knowing.

Gradually the routine of guiding became so much a part of my life, the packing up and heading out into the bush, the adventure of meeting new parties and the happy reunions when old ones returned, that after a time it seemed as though I had never done anything else.

But there was something more I got from them—their feeling for the land itself. This I have never forgotten, and when cities bear too heavily, I remember the guides of the Quetico-Superior who had no subtleties or hidden purposes, to whom the idea of contracts and influence was foreign, and who were as genuine and down to earth as the rocky shores of the waterways they followed.

Much of the joy of those years was exploring new country, and many of the first trips were just that. Once leaving Darkey Lake north of the border we decided to follow a river running out of it toward the northwest on a hunch that eventually it would drain into one of the larger lakes such as Lac la Croix. At first there were a series of rocky rapids so shallow we had to wade most of the time, the stream crisscrossed and crowded by heavy alder growth and willows. Gradually it slowed into a broad muskeg, winding on and on into the distance, but the water was deep and we paddled around bend after bend. In one shallow place grown with water lilies, we saw five moose, and later twelve, proof they had never been disturbed. As we approached they paid no attention, and only when we were close did they deign to move out of our way. We finally reached a beautiful lake without a name, and following its outlet, emerged in Martin's Bay of La Croix.

Usually it was a different kind of exploring. Whenever we were windbound by rain or storms or when I was not too sure what lay ahead, I would leave the canoes and head for some distant hill to climb a tree and look for a spot of blue. Sometimes the men would come with me, enjoying the adventure as much as I. Once we saw the blue we returned to the canoes, then with saws and axes cut a trail. Those portages were often long and rugged, and frequently they led to little lakes that had no outlets or connection with waters beyond, but the excitement of standing on a shore none of us had ever seen before more than made up for the backbreaking labor of getting there.

This exploring gave me an urge that has never been completely satisfied, a need that carried me into the far north hundreds and finally thousands of miles from home. I realize now what a tremendous privilege it was, how fortunate I was, to have lived at a time when there was still new and unmapped country. To know what thousands of early Americans had done gave me new perspective on the value of wilderness.

Young men today are little different from those who manned the wagon trains or struck off on treks into the unknown only a century ago; they still need to test themselves. To be tough in sinew and mind and scornful of discomfort and ease, no matter if times have changed, is a common asset of youth, and when inexhaustible energy can be spent in travel through relatively unknown country, the compensations are immeasurable. To climb mountains, go through impenetrable swamps and bogs, or cross deserts in the glare of a pitiless sun takes the same stamina as fighting the waves on great lakes, running dangerous rapids, or portaging over treacherous boulders. No matter where they find the challenges, this is what they need.

To handle an ax with power and precision, driving it into the same cut time after time, takes an eye and muscular control; to paddle without effort comes only after thousands of miles of using the whole body instead of the arms; to slice off a fillet neatly takes far more than a sharp blade—it takes the feel of the knife between the flesh and the skin, something one does not acquire overnight.

Buck Sletton once told me something when heading out into a driving rain. "Remember, young fellow," he said, with the old twinkle in his eyes, "remember, no matter how cold and wet you are, you're always warm and dry." I never forgot that advice, for in it was embodied a philosophy of life and a way of accepting the bush and all that it could mean. It involved not only a basic attitude, but the skills required to live comfortably under any and all conditions of wind and weather. To make a dry and pleasant camp in the face of a storm took more than taut tent ropes and knowing the lay of the land, it meant measuring up to a way of life all Americans once took for granted.

Exertion brings vital physiological reactions when there are worthwhile goals to achieve. Without weariness there can be no real appreciation of rest, without hunger no enjoyment of food; without the ancient responses to the harsh simplicities of the kind of environment that shaped mankind, a man cannot know the urges within him. Having known this during a period of life when I could satisfy these needs, I think I understand what wilderness can mean to the young men of today.

I was aware that the physical aspects of guiding were important, and that without a certain competence it could have been drudgery, but there were other influences that had as great an impact on my thinking. One of these was silence. To be sure, I had known it in the past, but not in the way I knew it as a guide, the cumulative effect of days and weeks on end. This was more than temporary release from noise, it was a primordial thing that seeped into the deepest recesses of the mind until mechanical intrusions were intolerable.

There were special places of deep silence, one a camp on a small island above the Pictured Rocks on Crooked Lake, a rocky, glaciated point looking toward the north, a high cliff on one side balanced by a mass of dark timber on the other. Each night we sat there looking down the waterway, listening to the loons filling the darkening narrows with wild reverberating music, but it was when they stopped that the quiet descended, an all-pervading stillness that absorbed all the sounds that had ever been. No one spoke. We sat there so removed from the rest of the world and with such a sense of complete remoteness that any sound would have been a sacrilege. The great mass of the cliff on one side, the gloom of the pines on the opposite shore, seemed to cup and hold it to the point where we were enveloped by a dark curtain that stifled all thought and feeling.

Then the loons would continue their calling, slashing the curtain as though with a knife, only to have it close again and be as darkly mysterious as before. Here was a deep awareness of ancient rhythms and the attunement men seek but seldom find.

There were many such spots; I found them in the morning and at high noon, as well as at dusk, for the time must be right not only for the place, but in the mind of him who listens. Kahshahpiwi had it in a canyon with the long gash of a waterway disappearing into the distance; Joyce, the hidden lake that seemed perpetually in flood; and Caribou at night when the stars were blazing and close enough to touch; but wherever it happened to be, it was the same, the all-engulfing silence of wilderness.

Since then I have searched for it everywhere and found it far from home. I have known it on the rim of the Grand Canyon at sunset when the colors changed from Chinese reds and burnished golds to the soft, dark purples of twilight, when looking down into the enormous chasm one catches the silence not only of the moment, but of the long eons while the Colorado River was cutting its way down to the very base of some of the oldest formations on earth.

Two years ago I walked out on the Sonoran desert at midnight with the stars so bright they seemed like planets close to earth. I had come to listen to the coyotes sing, smell the desert, and catch its feeling. On top of a hill I found a barren ledge from which I could look out across a valley and get a view of the heavens as well. Then began that strange, haunting medley of blended notes I had come to hear, first only one, then several, until the night was alive with music. Suddenly they stopped, and it was the same as when listening to the loons of the Quetico-Superior—the stillness descended.

I thought as I sat there that this was the quiet we knew

in our distant past when it was part of our minds and spirits. We have not forgotten and never will, though the scream and roar of jet engines, the grinding vibrations of cities, and the constant bombardment of electronic noise may seem to have blunted our senses forever. We can live with such clamor, it is true, in spite of what assails nervous systems attuned to the past, but we pay a price, and do so at our peril. I think the loss of quiet in our lives is one of the great tragedies of civilization, and to have known even for a moment the silence of the wilderness is one of our most precious memories.

Something else grew on me during those years of roaming and was never fully realized until I had been in the wilderness for a long time. This was the sense of timelessness and order. As I look back and see its first intimations, I understand my almost imperceptible involvement with a way of looking at life that truly had the power of slowing speed.

In town there were always deadlines, a host of things to do, but as soon as the canoes were in the water and heading out, the tempo changed. The guides slipped naturally into their old pattern; the city men, on the other hand, took longer, several days or a week, perhaps, and sometimes they never did succumb to the influence of natural events, which normally set the timetable for any expedition.

The coming of day and night, the eternal watching of the skies, sunrises and sunsets, the telltale story of winds in the maneuvering of clouds, the interwoven pattern of rain and mist, cycles of cold and warmth, even the changing vegetation—all these filtered into their consciousness as they did into mine. Once having lost our dependence on cosmic events, it was not always easy to regain it. While I had sensed its influence long before, the actual comprehension of time being endless and relative with all life flowing into its stream, took more than blind acceptance or a few hours' removal from civilization.

During some of my first trips I used to lay out a definite route of a hundred miles or more, with campsites strung conveniently along it. Not until I discovered I was simply following the routines of the men who had just left the cities and was robbing them of one of the real reasons for going into the bush did I finally abandon firm plans for some we could follow as we chose, living day by day with the vagaries of wind and weather, and not fretting if we failed to make a certain distance.

Once I tried to make McIntyre in one day from Basswood Lake going by way of Crooked, Robinson, and Sarah. Determined to get there by night, I had told my party about the wonderful fishing, trout on the reefs, walleyes off the campsite, a lake within easy reach swarming with largemouth bass. That day we fought the wind, were drenched with rain, passed up campsite after campsite thinking only of our goal, and by late afternoon were only on Caribou, ten miles away. Tempers were short, everyone thoroughly miserable, and regretfully I made camp, hoping to get an early start in the morning and come what may make our objective by noon.

The morning dawned cold and rainy, the wind was in our teeth. We could not go on, so I tried to make the best of it. Toward midafternoon and far too late for travel, the sun burst out; we took the canoes, left our sodden camp, and found a rocky reef with the finest fishing any of us had ever known. It was in the lee and away from the wind, and during the hour we spent there we were so intrigued we forgot all about McIntyre and decided to stay for an entire week.

That taught me a lesson: we could just as well have stopped in any one of the lakes on the way, and would have been happy. From then on my trips were different, and never again did I attempt the impossible to save my pride, or make a schedule more important than enjoyment. As time went on I knew the various routes more intimately and kept a store of surprises in mind, fishing holes, special lunch places, hidden campsites, and things to do when held up by weather. I was pleased to see how happy everyone was once the feeling of pressure was gone, and how much easier to adjust our plans. The wind might come up or change direction, the fish start hitting, the sun come out in time to air blankets and the outfit after several days of rain. Should someone discover ripe blueberries or a hill to climb, the departure might be delayed for an hour or a day.

With this kind of freedom tension and strain disap-

peared and laughter came easily. Men who hadn't sung a note
for years would suddenly burst into song, and at such times
I always thought of Buck and his feeling that loafing and
having fun was more important than fishing. When one
recalls the ages men lived as other creatures with no dependence on set routines, it is not surprising that once the
pattern has been broken, men react strongly. No wonder
when they return even for a short time to the ancient system to which they are really attuned, they know release.

Closely allied to the sense of unlimited time is the feeling of space. One is so much a part of the other it is impossible to separate them. No young guide imbued as I with the
romance and adventure of his work could comprehend the
real meaning of time and space, but as the years went
by, it penetrated my thinking, insidiously working its
magic, balancing the eons against the fury of an age of
technology.

As with silence, I have known this feeling in many
places, but more often, perhaps, on the lakes of the far north
or on the rolling tundras of the Arctic, or when looking across
ranges of mountains or the open sea. Airplane travel can
provide it, but a man flying high above the earth encased in
a metal cocoon is so removed from naturalness, it is usually
lost. In the wilderness and on the ground the old sensations
are there for the simple reason that this is the way man has
always known them. There is no other way, no short cuts or

artificial viewpoints. A man must see it as he has always done.

It is impossible to evaluate the importance of my guiding years and their influence on me, or to draw conclusions applicable to all, just as it is futile to list everything that affected me over the years. Ask any old-timer, voyageur, trapper, or guide why he stays in the bush and his answer is usually the same: freedom to come and go, freedom of thought and action. There is an old saying that it's easier to take a man out of the bush than to take the bush out of a man, and this I believe is true.

The bush is a complex of many joys—companionship on the trail, the thrills of exploration, the impact of silence, vastness, and infinity, the good feeling of doing something for its own sake without the spur of reward, the physical satisfaction of using bodies as they were meant to be used, and moving under one's own power, the complete naturalness of living out of doors.

Guiding gave me all this, and while it began half a century ago, its influence has continued, and the truths I found there in the Quetico-Superior have been strengthened and clarified. The guides and the men with whom I traveled sensed these truths, or caught occasional glimpses of them as I did, but it took many years to make them a part of me.

I always thought that Johnny Dahl, one of my guiding companions in those early days, had a special feel for the bush, and an air that set him apart—something in his stance and the way he walked and wore his outfit. Not long ago when we were reminiscing he confirmed it.

"You know," he said, "we were a special breed of cat in those days, and felt more about that country than we ever dared let on."

He hesitated a moment, then grinned a little self-consciously and added, "We were pretty good, and a little proud of being wilderness guides."

I look at wilderness now with profound respect, knowing it must be preserved as a retreat for harried mankind in a world hurtling toward what seems to be complete divorce from the past. Knowing what it means, I can better understand the vast complex of our needs and the longing for a way of life that with many is only a memory.

FROM

LISTENING POINT

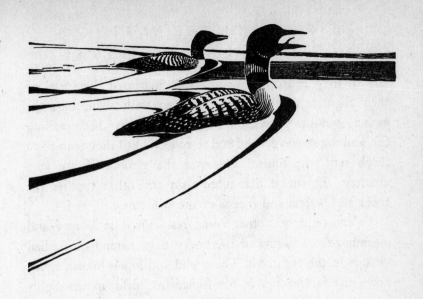

CHAPTER VIII

LAUGHING LOON

THE canoe was drifting off
the islands, and the time had come for the calling, that moment of magic in the north when all is quiet and the water
still iridescent with the fading glow of sunset. Even the shores
seemed hushed and waiting for that first lone call, and when
it came, a single long-drawn mournful note, the quiet was
deeper than before.

Above came a swift whisper of wings, and as the loons saw us they called wildly in alarm, increased the speed of their flight, and took their laughing with them into the gathering dusk. Then came the answers we had been waiting for, and the shores echoed and re-echoed until they seemed to throb with the music. This was the symbol of the lake country, the sound that more than any other typifies the rocks and waters and forests of the wilderness.

To me only one other compares with it in beauty and meaning, the howling of the husky dogs around the Indian villages in the far north. Their wild and lonely music epitomizes the far reaches of the Canadian Shield, means nights when northern lights are a blazing curtain along the horizon.

While the northern loon in startling black and white, with its necklace of silver and jet and five-foot spread of wings, is of great interest scientifically, it is the calling that all remember. Whoever has heard it during spring and summer never forgets the wild laughing tremolo of the reverberating choruses.

One such night is burned into my memory. It was moonlight, the ice had just gone out, and the spring migration was in full swing. Loons were calling everywhere, not only on Knife but on adjacent lakes, and the night was full of their music from sunset until dawn. The echoes kept the calling going until it was impossible at times to tell which was real. While I listened it seemed to me that in that confused medley of sounds was a certain harmony as though major chords were being held for periods of time. It may have been imagination, but I have heard hints of it at other times as well. On this night there was no mistake, for the calling blended with the echoes until the illusion was complete.

The weirdest call of all is the yodel somewhat similar to the break in voice and the clear bugle-like note used by humans in calling across wide valleys in the Alps. This is the danger call used when a canoe is approaching a nesting area or when invasion is imminent. It can start all the loons within hearing, and when the yodeling blends with tremolo they are really making music.

The third call is the wail often mistaken for the howl of a wolf, and of much the same quality. It rises and falls in pitch and is used when a mate is calling for relief from its brooding on the nest or when signaling the young. Just that morning we heard it among the islands. We had been watching a pair swim slowly around the little bay where they had nested, with a lone chick riding sedately upon the back of one of them. When they saw us, they gave their warning calls at once, for that lone chick riding so grandly around the bay and no more than a day or two off the nest was far too small to fend for itself. We paddled toward them while the calling grew more and more intense, came at last directly between the parents and their young one, which now was trying desperately to dive. A week old it would have been able to submerge and swim for fifty feet or more, but this little chap was at our mercy and the parents were aware of its danger. At times they came almost within touching distance and tried to draw us away with the old ruse of pretending to have a broken wing and thus easy to catch. How they floundered and threw themselves about. When their enticements failed to work, they approached again, rearing up on their tails and uttering loud cries as they balanced there and all but treading water before flopping forward onto their breasts. The performance was repeated over and over again. They screamed and hooted and yodeled and gave the laughing call, but to no avail, while the chick, now confused and thoroughly frightened, swam hopelessly beside the canoe. Other loons in the vicinity swiftly joined the commotion, and the entire area was in turmoil.

Deciding they had been frightened too much, we turned and paddled back to the point, but for a long time after we had gone the calling continued. It was not surprising they were alarmed, for this lone chick brought out all of their protective instincts for the season of mating and nesting. Seldom owning more than two and often only one because of predation, they found in that last chick their whole excuse for being.

Just after the ice was out we had watched that pair come into the bay, stake out their nesting area, and repel invaders whenever they approached. One day we watched the courtship. They came toward each other slowly and, as they neared, dipped their bills rapidly in the water and just as rapidly flipped them out again. This was followed by several short swift dives, exaggerated rolling preens and stretchings such as only loons seem able to do. Suddenly they broke away from such intimacy, raced off across the water, striking the surface with powerful wing beats in a long curving path that eventually led back to where they had started. All during this time they indulged in the laughing call. Sometimes in the ecstasy of display they reared high on their tails as they did when their chick was endangered, struck their snowy breasts violently on the water, then raced again around the bay. Only once did we see this, but shortly afterward the mating was over and then we found the nest in a tussock of grass on a little swampy island close to shore and facing the open water. It was placed so they could slip off swiftly and reach the deeps should danger come behind them from the shore. The two olive-brown and somewhat speckled eggs were soon laid in a small shallow depression in the grass that was built up during the days of incubation until it was a concave little mound, each mate doing its share while it sat there, pecking and adding a grass blade at a time from the vegetation within reach.

A couple of weeks later one of the eggs was destroyed by some prowler, possibly a mink, a crow or a muskrat. The remaining egg now took all of their attention, and they guarded it jealously every moment of the day and night. If this had been stolen too, it would have meant a new nest and possibly another hatching.

Scientists say that in half the nests only one hatches out, and that the low rate of survival accounts for the fact that loons are never numerous. If two individuals reproduce themselves after their third year, then things are going well.

It is surprising in view of the high mortality rate that populations remain as steady as they do, that, in spite of predation, loons are found on almost every lake in the north.

One afternoon we sat on the point watching a flock of them playing on the open water. They had been there as a group since midsummer, bachelor loons and pairs that had not nested or had lost their eggs. Now free of responsibilities, these thwarted birds gathered each morning and spent the day together in the open. It may have been that the fishing was good in that particular spot, but I am tempted to believe they got together for a companionship that took the place of nests and young.

Suddenly one of the group called and then all together until the channel before us was again full of sound. Excited by their own music, they chased one another madly across the water, returning always to the place they had left. Toward dusk the flock began to disband, single birds first and then pairs flying back, no doubt, to their abandoned nesting areas. Sometime in the morning they would drift back again by ones and twos to spend the day together as they do on many of the larger lakes all summer long.

A pair flew close to the point and settled in the bay off the beach, and we watched them diving there for minnows, timing them to see how long they could stay submerged. Seldom did one stay under for more than half a minute, but there are records of dives as long as two and three minutes in duration. Some have been recorded even longer than that, but such observers may have failed to see a partial emergence for air. They are wonderful divers and swimmers, can pursue and overtake the swiftest of fish, and it has been said a loon can dive at the flash of a gun and be under water before the bullet strikes.

They can also submerge gradually, can control specific gravity possibly by a compression of feathers and expulsion of air from the lungs until the body is approximately the same weight as the water. All divers have a high tolerance for carbon dioxide, and oxygen needs are met, not from free air in the lungs, but from the oxyhemoglobin and oxymyoglobin stored in the muscles, substances responsible for the dark color of flesh in most waterfowl. This explains the diving, the gradual sinking from sight, and the fact that they have been caught on fishermen's set lines in Lake Superior at depths of two hundred feet.

Once I sat in a canoe at Lower Basswood Falls and watched a loon fishing in the rapids not fifty feet away. Suddenly the bird dove and swam directly under the canoe not two feet below the surface. The wings were held tightly at the sides and the legs the sole means of locomotion. When a young chick is learning to swim beneath the surface it uses both legs and wings, a reversion perhaps to the days of its reptilian ancestors; a habit generally abandoned, however, when it becomes adult.

It was now much too dark to see and we left our loons for the light and warmth of the cabin, but in the morning we watched them again. The pair had stayed close to the bay during the night and now were swimming around in the sunshine, getting ready to join the gathering flock on the open lake. We watched them, the brilliant black-and-white markings on their backs, saw one preen, rolling over on its side exposing the silvery-white breast until it glittered and shone in the morning sun. The other rose to its full height, flapped its wings vigorously, and settled down again. Then both dove with scarcely a ripple to mark their descent and soon were far past the point, heading for the rendezvous.

Some say that loons eat too many fish and should be reduced in numbers, but as the population on most lakes is small, with usually only one or two per square mile of the area, this is a ridiculous assumption. To be sure, they do eat fish, but, like most predators of the type, they also eat insects, mollusks, crustacea, and even vegetation. We can well afford to keep them, for their aesthetic value far outweighs any other consideration. Without the music of their calling and the sight of them on the open water, the lakes of the north would never be the same.

A pair flew overhead, and we heard plainly the whistle of their wings, watched the slow and powerful beats as they headed across the lake. As they passed the gathering flock they gave the tremolo once and then settled down with the rest. I had hoped they might do what I had seen them do in the past, glide into the waiting group with wings set and held in a motionless V above their backs. Once I had seen them come in that way on Kekekabic, approaching the lake like seaplanes about to land in a long unbroken glide from the top of the ridge to the water's surface.

But, while they are strong flyers and can swim and dive as few birds can, they are absolutely helpless on land, and only once have I seen one more than twenty feet from water. I was coming across a portage with a canoe on my back, and there, to my amazement, was a loon standing bolt upright in the center of the trail. I was so startled by the apparition in black and white that its scream of alarm almost made me drop the canoe. The bird turned and literally hurled itself toward the shore, half flying, swimming and running on its ridiculously tiny legs. With a wild water-choked yelp it plunged into the shallows and out to diving depth and swiftly disappeared. That explained why nests are always close to the shore. Loons must be able to slide instantly into the water, cannot waste precious moments struggling over land. No creature is clumsier out of its element than this great diver of the north.

The sound of a whippoorwill means an orange moon coming up in the deep south; the warbling of meadowlarks the wide expanses of open prairies with the morning dew still upon them; the liquid notes of a robin before a rain the middle west and east; the screaming of Arctic terns the marshes of the far north. But when I hear the wild rollicking laughter of a loon, no matter where I happen to be, it means only one place in the world to me—the wilderness lake country and Listening Point.

CHAPTER IX

KING'S POINT

THE scraggly little pine on
the end of the point belongs to the memory of Walt Hurn.
It is bent and twisted, had once been flattened against the
rock by some storm on the past, only to point upward again.
Now it is anchored in a cleft of the greenstone, having only
a few tortured branches that have survived the winds. They

are gnarled and out of shape, but hold their tufts of needles defiantly against the sky. The little pine is part of Listening Point and of my memories as well. It belongs there, would be out of place in a fertile protected valley. Conditioned by the past, it can never grow tall and straight like the rest, but will always reveal its background.

Walt Hurn, once Canadian ranger at King's Point just to the north, was like that pine, for he too had weathered the storms and in the process had become just as gnarled, indestructible and indigenous. Although it has been thirty years since I checked in with him on my way to Quetico Provincial Park as a young guide, I can still see the great spare shoulders bent desperately over a report, the rootlike fingers moving slowly across the page with a tiny stub of a pencil all but lost between them, fingers used to rocks and boulders, to ax work and the heavy packs of portages. During those days he was King's Point, part of the log ranger station nestled under the tall Norways, part of the brooding cliffs of Ranger's Bay behind and the broad sweep of water toward Jackfish and the outlet. The fluttering Union Jack was more than a symbol of authority and an outpost of the Empire. To me it meant Walt Hurn. Like the gale-beaten pine beside me, he belonged to the Canadian bush, or so I thought, a ranger of the old school who had taken over his post long before anyone ever thought of tourists or wilderness canoe trips and when blank spaces on the maps still meant the unexplored. When he used to talk about going outside, I never took him seriously. All woodsmen talked that way, but when the time came there was always some excuse for staying on.

"Someday," he'd say, "I'm going to turn in my ranger's badge and head for Merrie England, buy me a little garden spot near the coast, and raise the prettiest flowers on the island."

I used to laugh at him. "Walt," I would say, "you know you couldn't stand it over there. This is your country," and then we would walk around and look at all he had done there, and all that time I did not know how he felt.

To me the idea that he could transplant himself to some pocket-sized garden plot with clipped hedgerows after knowing the wilds and the freedom of the north seemed incongruous. I could have as easily imagined taking the twisted pine from its rocky holdfast and planting it in the rich soil of Kew Gardens outside London.

Because I was young and did not know that men are unlike trees, that within them is more than fiber and resin and the will to live, I thought it would be that way with Walt. I did not understand that what had made his lonely station different from any other in Quetico Park and possibly in the whole of Canada was a core of loyalty to another way of life that the wilds could never quite erase, that in everything he did his memories came to life. This was the real Walt Hurn and a man I did not know.

All of the crew of hard-bitten young guides felt the same about King's Point. There is something different about jumping-off places, no matter where they happen to be. Whenever one leaves security and says good-by to the familiar, events seem to be more sharply etched. People stand out as types, and everything is colored more vividly. But even though we were used to such places all over the map, Walt Hurn and his station were different from the rest. Now that I look back and realize what the old ranger did there, it all fits into a pattern, from the way he treated us to the many things he did that made King's Point what it was.

No matter if we had been gone for weeks or months and this was our first exciting touch with civilization, he never so much as lifted an eyebrow or let on that our arrivals were anything out of the ordinary. We were puzzled at times, for coming out of the bush is no light experience when you are young and full of the joy of life. Now I know it was part of the whole picture he had created there, part of a background of quiet conservatism we knew nothing about. To him our adventures were all in the day's work.

To eyes that for long had seen nothing but the wild, his little spot of grassy turf between the beach and the cabin was exciting. It wasn't a clipped lawn or laid out in any particular way, just a bit of bluegrass that had taken root beneath the Norways, a tough bit of sod that somehow never needed cutting. We spent many hours there waiting for a tow, lying on our backs looking up through the tops of the pines, pure luxury after the rocks of portages and the torrent-washed bottoms of river beds.

One of the many things that impressed us at King's Point was its order and cleanness. Starting down at the beach with its white sand and gravel and its two trim canoe rests, this

cleanness spread up over the point itself, took in the woodpile, the toolshed, the cabin, clear back into the timber. Even
under the trees not a cone seemed out of place.

But the log cabin was something to see. Just being clean
would never do. The floor was always scrubbed snowy
white, and no paint or varnish was ever allowed to touch it.
Even though it would have saved much labor and preserved
the wood, we had a feeling that Walt considered such artifice
a sign of weakness and lack of character.

Because of his passion for order, there was about King's
Point a perennial Sunday-morning freshness. Sometimes we
thought he overdid it, that there was no excuse for having a
floor so white we felt we must take off our boots before
stepping inside, but all of this had a place there and an effect
on every one of us. We never dreamed of arriving without
having washed our torn wilderness outfits and shaved our
beards. King's Point demanded nothing less.

You would never believe that a garden patch up there in
the wilds meant very much, but it did—more, in fact, than
most of us ever cared to admit. Even though we did not
know its real meaning to Walt Hurn, the impact of it was in-
escapable, and after each trip we looked forward to seeing it.

Coming out of the bush where all vegetation runs riot to
suddenly find clean gravel walks, vegetables in straight rows
and a profusion of flowers, when for a long time we had
known only muskeg, rocks, and timber, did something to us.

I used to walk between the beds back of the cabin, tramp-
ing almost reverently down the paths in my hobnailed boots,

marveling at the sky blue of larkspur and delphinium, the burnt orange of poppies, and the crimson of hollyhocks and zinnias. Somehow up there those colors were a miracle; not that I was a flower-lover particularly, but order and color were such a change from what I had seen. Back home I would have taken it for granted, but on King's Point it was entirely different.

A little pansy bed lay right in front of the cabin. It had stakes driven all around it to keep out the rabbits, and all season long it was filled with bloom. I could never resist the rich velvet flowers that grew there; coming up from the beach I always picked one to wear in my buttonhole, and if I failed to make my choice, soon after my arrival Walt reminded me. He was pleased that I noticed his tiny bed.

The luxuriousness of his flowers and garden was due to the compost pile beside the cabin, and to him compost was more precious than anything on the point. No bit of garbage was ever wasted, no leaves or grass burned, no fish entrails, carcasses, or offal of any kind were buried elsewhere. Everything went into that soft black mound.

"Humus," he used to say, crumbling the stuff in his great hard palm, smelling it, gloating at its dark richness. "There's the stuff that makes 'em grow, there's where you get the color."

The compost heap was typical of Walt and in a way was the key to everything he did. His creation back in the wilds of the border country was a bit of the beauty of the old England he had left behind.

There were many other things that over the years worked themselves into our memories: the deep-dish blueberry pies he baked, the sourdough pancakes we had beside the crackling kitchen stove in the dark of a morning, stormy nights when we'd roll up on the floor and listen to the crash of thunder and the waves down at the beach. Then, too, the rocky islands coasting the bay in front, and the roar on quiet nights of Basswood Falls on the route to Lac la Croix.

Yes, there was much to remember, for King's Point was beautiful even as it is today, but it was not a matter of beauty alone or the fact that here was a garden in the wilderness and that it was clean and immaculate. The important thing, I realize now, was that Walt Hurn was there, and it never occurred to any of us that someday it would change.

That was why it was such a shock one fall to learn that he was coming down, that he had turned in his badge and was leaving the Service just as he had said he would and was going back to Merrie England. Somehow we could not believe it, for it seemed to our young minds an unnatural thing to do. The day he was scheduled to come down from King's Point was a blue-gold one in October. We were down at the dock on Fall Lake, had been there most of the morning talking about the tourist season just past, of guiding prospects for the coming year, and watching the head of the lake for the first telltale spout of spray.

"There she comes," someone said.

We looked up toward the narrows, saw a launch coming around the point, spewing the waves before it, slapping its way gaily into the morning blow. It bore down the channel and headed directly toward us. One passenger, a pack, and a couple of big boxes on the deck, and that was all.

Until the last moment we hoped that the launch would be empty, but now we knew we were wrong. There was no mistaking the broad-shouldered frame, the weathered old hat, or the way he stood. He waved once, got ready for the landing. The bow swung in with an extra flourish, gears ground in reverse, and the boat warped into position. Willing hands tied it fast.

After we had his outfit on the dock, Walt stood for a moment looking up the lake toward the Four Mile Portage across American Point.

"Well, boys," was all he said, "it's the last time. Now for Merrie England," and the old twinkle was in his eyes—just as matter-of-fact and casual as that, just the way he used to say good-by in the old days, no fuss or sentiment, merely a checking out as though he would be back in a couple of weeks.

A truck was waiting at the road. He climbed in, waved once, and suddenly was gone, and with him the King's Point we had known.

The twisted little pine rustled in a sudden breeze, and then the wind came strongly and the turf with its layer of brown needles and silvery caribou moss moved gently above the root and the crevice of the rock. It would always bring me memories of Walt Hurn and the days when I thought that he too belonged to the rugged land of the Quetico.

CHAPTER X

THE PORTAGE

THE portage lay in the end of the bay, and there a battered white sign was nailed to a tree. As the canoe slipped beside a log we stepped into the shallows and lifted out the packs. The sign was broken in half, torn no doubt by a curious bear, weathered and beaten by the wind, but on it were the names of voyageurs who had gone before.

I stood for a long time looking at that sign as I have looked at hundreds in the wilderness lake country here and far to the north, and marveling as I always do that somehow I had arrived at a known and definite point on the map. That morning the portage had seemed far away from the point. There had been miles of open water, narrows and islands to traverse, and now, at last, here it was exactly where it was supposed to be.

The trail was narrow, no more than a foot in width, for men, like animals, in the wilds make little paths. It was carpeted with pine needles and the leaves of aspen and birch, packed hard by the feet of generations of travelers. It led between rocks, around hummocks, skirting wet places, using logs for bridges where the muck was soft, over windfalls and around clumps of blocking trees. This primitive path was part of the great network that laces together the waterways, a connecting link between two lakes, but in its simplicity and the way it threaded through the woods it was typical of all the wilderness trails in the world.

The first man who found his way through here had followed perhaps the trails of moose or caribou, for they also travel from lake to lake, but because they seldom follow the shortest route he was forced to branch off and head for the closest point of the shore. No doubt he climbed a tree or a ridge to get his bearings, then returned and blazed his way or broke off branches to guide him back.

The next man through followed the marked trail with more ease, broke more branches, slashed a few more blazes on the trees, might even have cut a windfall blocking the way. From then on each traveler improved the portage a little more until at last it was as definite and direct as the terrain would allow. After many years of use, someone with more ambition than the rest chopped out the great logs that men had scrambled over and finally tacked a sign on a tree near the water so that canoes coming in would see it from the lake.

This portage was primitive, as all such trails are, the result of steady improvement by all who came that way, and dedicated to a type of use that belonged to the wilderness. To straighten out the bends and loops that had become a part of it because of obstacles avoided, to remove all natural hazards and even to mark it too well would have taken something from it, just as an old and winding road changes in character when all the curves are eliminated in the interest of speed.

For countless thousands of years men have followed such trails. It is instinctive to pack across them, and you bend and weave, adjust your weight and balance, do all the things your subconscious experience tells you to do without realizing exactly what is happening. In the low places your feet feel for the rocks and tussocks of grass, for the sunken logs that keep you from bogging down. You approach them as a horse approaches a bridge, with the same awareness of danger. Over the rocks and beside a rapids where a slip might plunge you into a torrent or over a cliff, your feet are your eyes as they have always been where the going is rough.

Once I followed one of the traces along the crest of the

downs in the south of England. It was high above the villages and above the woods, wound its way along the tops of the open hills as it had for many thousands of years. This was one of the trails of the ancient tribes that inhabited the island long before the Romans came, long before any of the roads they built. The Celts traveled high, the better to watch their enemies. Up there along the crest they could see far and the going was clear. The men who followed those traces picked their routes of travel like wolves who follow open ridges in the north. Along them are the Druid circles and ancient places of worship and sacrifice, and, like portages, they too are narrow and winding and as natural as the game trails they might have been during England's past.

There are also the walking trails across the fields of England, the stiles over fences and hedgerows, trails that because of their historic value are recognized as legal highways that cannot be blocked by owners of the land. These traces and foot paths were the first roads. Dignified by tradition and centuries of use, they are part of the cultural background of the people.

On the North American continent these traces are also in evidence, not only the portages between lakes and along the river systems but trails through great areas of terrain. To these belong the Iroquois War Road from New England to the south, the Natchez Trace from Tennessee almost to the Gulf of Mexico, the Wilderness Road of Daniel Boone, the Oregon Trail, and the Santa Fe, all walking trails for warriors and pioneers.

In time many of them became roads and later the arterials of today. Cities were built along them, just as the villages of England strung themselves like beads along the ancient traces of the downs. Most of those old trails are gone now, but, for those who know where to look, remnants can still be found and from the soaring crests of the new highways one can catch the vision of the men who marked them first.

I have known portages all over the country, the short un-important ones not rating a name, the difficult ones often-times of great historic interest. There is Grand Portage, once gateway to the northwest, the nine-mile carry around the brawling rapids of the Pigeon River where it empties into Lake Superior; Staircase Portage just above, where voya-geurs built a wooden stairway down a steep cliff; Frog Skin Portage from the Churchill to the Sturgeon Weir, where the Sioux as a mark of derision stretched a frogskin and hung it there to show the Crees, who had not learned to stretch a beaverhide, that this was how it was done. The legends about them are many, for it was here men met on the long routes they must follow in the north.

I thought of these things as I tossed the canoe onto my shoulders and started across the portage. Countless feet had trod it smooth long before I came. During the logging days part of it had been used as a tote road, but now it was grown to brush and trees again. It is a long carry and uphill most of the way and I thought I could make it without a stop, but near its crest I weakened, placed the bow of the canoe in the crotch of a birch, and rested. Then almost imperceptibly the trail led down the ridge, and it was then I caught the first sight of blue, just a glimmer through the trees but enough to take away the weariness and fill me with the same old joy I had known thousands of times in the past, an elation that never grows old and never will as long as men carry canoes and packs along the waterways. In spite of the labor, it is this that makes portaging worth while. There is no substitute. If someone transports your outfit for you, it is lost. It colors your entire attitude, makes each lake reached mean infinitely more. It is exactly like climbing a mountain. You could be dropped there by helicopter or view it from a low-flying plane, but unless you have climbed cliffs, scaled precipices, and inched your way upward, fighting for breath, you have no understanding of the satisfaction of the first long look into space. So it is with portages and the first sight of glorious blue through the trees. When I dropped my canoe at last into the water and stood there puffing and blowing and looking down the expanse of the lake, my feeling of accomplishment was one that had been earned.

But just walking across a portage has its compensations too. In a canoe, even though you slip quietly along the shores, you still cannot achieve the feeling of intimacy that is yours on the ground. There you hear sounds that are lost on the water, see things that until then have been hidden. After hours of paddling, a portage brings new muscles into use, and how delightful to rest with your back against the canoe, doing the aimless things one does when there is nothing to think about and rest is the greatest luxury on earth.

Such an interlude was one at the end of the McAree Portage, where I sat and idly scuffed the moss with the toe of my boot. I felt something hard and, thinking it might be a root, kicked it loose. To my surprise, it was an old knife, heavily rusted, with the horn handle partly gone. I scraped off the rust and there was the mark IXL, one of the trade knives carried by Indians and voyageurs. Dropped perhaps during a meal or after skinning a beaver, there it had lain until I kicked it free. That knife is now in the cabin, a reminder to me not only of the days of the fur trade but of the delight of a resting-place on the portage from McAree to the island-studded reaches of Lac la Croix.

No one in the Quetico-Superior country has arrived, how- ever, until he has made the Kashapiwi Portage, a mile of the most rugged terrain along the border. It starts from Yum Yum Lake and is fairly level at first, then goes down into a swampy beaver flowage where in the spring the water may be waist deep, and then over a high and mountainous ridge. The view from that ridge of the knifelike gash that is Kasha- piwi and its high shores, with the realization that only those who are willing to take the punishment of that grueling trail may see it, is reward enough.

Some lakes have no portages between them because most travelers follow major routes. Between these routes, how- ever, are waterways unknown and unexplored. An itinerant hunter or trapper may have worked his way into them, but a blazed trail without continual use grows swiftly back to brush and trees. Sometimes when exploring it is necessary to cut a trail into one of these waters off the known paths of travel, an experience modern canoeists may still enjoy. In the early days before aerial surveys and photographs, before dependable maps were even dreamed of, there were many blank spaces where the country was a challenge.

Years ago I was camped on Robinson Lake just north of the border, determined to explore the country toward the northwest. One day we pushed into a long bay and thought we were on the route to the lakes I had heard were there. At one point we lifted the canoe around a log that blocked our passage through a narrows into another lake, but found it was just a swampy bay of Robinson itself and that we would have to try again.

The following morning we climbed a high hill in the far east end of Dart Lake and then a tall pine that gave us a sweep of the country to the north. There, as I had hoped, was a single spot of blue nestled between the ridges. We spent the morning blazing a portage through a swamp and did not finish the carry until late afternoon. On the shore of our little spot of blue at last, we were thrilled because it was wild and unknown and we were on our way. Three deer stood in the shallows at the far end, spots of orange in the last level rays of the sun. A blue heron flapped lazily away, and signs of moose were along the shore. A rocky ledge loomed beyond the narrows. We would camp there if we could find a level spot and in the morning head for the north and the waters we now were sure lay before us.

We loaded in the packs and paddled out into deeper water, and a school of bass followed us unafraid. At the narrows a windfall blocked our way, so we beached the canoe and walked around it. Then suddenly I was overcome with a powerful sense of having been there before, and with good reason, for there in the sand was the clear sharp imprint of a boot. We looked at it in shocked and incredulous amazement just as Robinson Crusoe must have done when he saw the track of Friday on the sands of his lonely island. Then we knew the truth. That footprint was where I had stepped out the day before, and the channel was the one we had explored out of Robinson Lake. Neither of us said a word; we just carried the canoe around the log and paddled back to the campsite we had left with such high hopes that morning. We had made a complete circle, cut a portage that never again would be used by man, but all was not lost, for we had known the thrill of exploration and, until the final realization of our error, the excitement of seeing country for the first time.

But of all the portages I have known, the one I most often dream about when I am far from the canoe country is along a knifelike ledge of rock between two gorges on the Saganagons. On my first trip down that river I camped there on a tiny level shelf of rock on a night that was full of the thunder of rapids and falls on either side. That place made such an impression on my young mind it has become endowed with mystery and I have only to close my eyes to hear its music.

And there are many more, those that wind between the boles of great trees and those with far vistas from the highlands with their smooth glaciated rocks like pavements through the woods. There are short delightful ones, merely interludes between the paddling, and long hard ones from one watershed to another. But always they are gateways to adventure, meeting-places for voyageurs, punctuation marks between the long blue sentences of lakes across the maps.

FROM

RUNES OF THE NORTH

CHAPTER XI

GHOST CAMPS OF THE NORTH

THE *voyageurs* of our expedition had battled their way up the Camsell River from the height of land above Great Slave toward the barren bleakness of Great Bear. It was a time of rain and cold; the winds off the arctic ice never ceased. The terrain had grown more and more rugged, and each day we fought the waves, dodged behind islands, and skirted dangerous promontories we could not avoid. We ran what rapids our canoes could take, but when they were bad, portaged, for in that icy water we dared not take a chance.

The hills were almost mountainous now, great glaciated masses of rock, the ragged growth of spruce all but gone except along the lake shores and in the valleys of connecting streams. It was a savage land and full of beauty, even where the fires had been and billowing ridges of granite lay bare to pitiless gales.

Not a soul had we seen since our trip began, no Indians or vestiges of their camps. They had migrated long ago to the milder climate of the Mackenzie Valley to the west. There was more game to hunt, riverboats and barges passed constantly on their way to Norman Wells and Aklavik, and activity was never lacking around the Hudson's Bay posts and the missions. The Camsell lay deserted as though the glacier had just retreated. So accustomed had we been to seeing no one, it was with great excitement we saw something strange on the opposite shore of a lake on the way to Hottah.

We got out the glasses and studied it intently. It was a wrecked plane, a DC-3 lying at a crazy angle against the bank, with one wing much lower then the other, behind it several cabins, possibly a mine or some trader's outfit. Quickly we changed course and headed toward it. That low wing meant trouble and in the north a downed plane is never ignored. As we neared, we studied it again. There was no mistake, the craft was lying close against the rocky shore.

We pushed swiftly now and on the way passed a little island, its bare surface completely covered with a mat of orange lichen. I could not resist taking a color shot as we passed, a spot of orange with tufts of golden grass against the leaden background of the lake. We landed at what had once been a dock. The planks were broken now, the piling loose and tilted. The aircraft was only a shell, one motor gone, the other a wreck, the interior stripped and dismantled. The loading door hung on its hinges and creaked in the wind. The tipped wing was supported by a crib of logs. There was nothing to salvage, it would stay there for a long time, gleaming against the shore. We walked up the well-beaten trail to one of the cabins, opened the unlocked door and stepped inside.

This was the cook shack, the table set for twenty men. Bread and butter were still there, meat, mashed potatoes, jelly and jam. A pumpkin pie with one wedge missing stood at the end. The gravy bowl was full, the sliced bread and cake hard. Nothing had been touched or molested, no signs of squirrels, mice, or rats, no decay or spoilage. It was as though the men had left the day before in the midst of a meal.

I went into the kitchen, its shelves stocked with food, hundreds of dollars worth, enough to keep the crew going for months, tinned supplies precious in this far country, vegetables, strawberries, peaches, tinned meats, and sausage. In a back lean-to hung a dried up haunch of moose, a hide, and a slab of bacon. Shining utensils hung on the walls: pots and pans, knives, skillets, spoons. Nothing was out of place.

We left and walked into the next building, the office of the engineer and superintendent. On a drafting table was an unfinished sketch of the mining property, a file for letters and plans. I thumbed through the file; the last letter was dated at the close of the Korean war. A uranium mine, it had been discontinued when rich prospects close to civilization no longer warranted its operation. A mahogany box contained a new theodolite in a velvet case. It had never been used and was worth a great deal of money. Surveying instruments stood in a corner, drill bits, flat iron strips and bars were laid neatly on separate racks.

The men's quarters and bunkhouses were the same, items of personal equipment, gloves, shirts, rain gear and boots, all left behind in the hurry of departure. On a small table beside one of the bunks I picked up a cluster of quartz crystals. Some were stained with iron, some the color of old rose, others close to amethyst. They were clear and well shaped. On one crystal was a deposit of silver, between two other faces a tiny speck of the same orange lichen we had seen on the little island in crossing the lake. Since it was a perfect specimen, I picked it up, dropped it into my pocket. It is before me now as I write and brings the scene of that abandoned mining camp back to me.

We returned to the cook shack, sat down at the table with the uneasy feeling that the men who had been there last were still around, the cook busying himself in the kitchen before his stove, the *cookee* bringing in the food, seeing the gravy was hot, the teapot full. None of us spoke. This was a place of ghosts. We closed the door carefully so no animals would get in. Ten years, or a hundred, it would make little difference in that frigid climate.

Back in the engineer's office, we picked up the theodolite and placed it carefully in one of the half-empty packs. It was very heavy, but none of us could bear the thought of leaving it behind. We would drop it off eventually at Eldorado on Great Bear.

We took some tinned fruit and meat, went back to the canoes, pushed off toward the lichen-covered rock and east toward our rendezvous on Great Bear. As we rounded the last point, I turned and looked back. There was the gleam of silver, behind it the dark cluster of cabins, the table still set, the engineer's shack, the bunkhouses, the hopes and dreams of men who had lived and perhaps died there. Too costly to fly out, the camp was left as many others were in the far reaches of the north. Some day, should the demand warrant, it might open again, but now it was better lost and forgotten.

Not until we reached Eldorado did we know the story, how one of the supply planes had gone through the crust of spring ice with one of its pontoons. One wing had been almost sheared, an engine ruined, the fuselage twisted out of shape—no casualties, just one of those accidents that happen to bush pilots all over the north. The men had saved what they could, but there the wreck would stay until the elements corroded the aluminum and it finally sank into the water and muck along the shore.

Two years later I came across another ghost camp almost a thousand miles to the southeast. It was during the course of a caribou survey where the endless tundra bordering Hudson Bay meets the scraggly line of the Taiga, that land of stunted spruce, muskeg, and caribou moss that extends not only through our own north but across all of Siberia as well. The migration was on, and we were flying in to join a research party tagging the caribou in an attempt to determine how they moved.

From the air, Duck Lake Post of the Hudson's Bay Company looked like any other on the tundra, or for that matter anywhere in the north, a white building with a red roof, a cluster of storage sheds and shacks, a warehouse for furs and supplies, canoe racks, a little dock. Built on a bare point of land between Duck Lake and Nejanilini, it once served the scattered bands of Swampy Crees and even some of the Eskimo of the Wolverine-Seal River country, as far west as Nueltin and east to Hudson Bay. It was isolated enough so travelers seldom came and, when they did, it was a momentous event.

But this time there was no running about, no waving or frantic preparations for our arrival, no smoke from the chimneys, no tents or shelters around the post or canoes pulled up on the shore, no dogs straining at their chains and howling their hearts out in the excitement of our landing. Not a soul was to be seen anywhere, only a lone fox streaking across the point for the cover of the willow fringe beyond. We swung low to be sure of the approach, buzzed the little gray deserted church across the bay. It was weather-beaten, with the windows gone and grass growing around its steps. The cross was at an angle leaning away from the wind.

We landed a quarter of a mile out in the lake, taxied cautiously to the dock. The outer cribbing was broken by the ice, the planking torn apart. We had difficulty in warping the Norseman into position because of sharp, protruding rocks, but finally tied it fast and walked up the trail to the main building. The Hudson's Bay Company sign was gone, nothing to indicate ownership. The store was still in good repair but the shelves were empty. I went into the kitchen and started a fire in the stove. It smoked at first, but after the debris and soot burned out it drew well. The coffee pot, kettles, and skillets were clean and we used them rather than get out our own. Supper was served in the small dining room where the factor had eaten many times with guests who came to visit. Beds and bunks were still in place in the attic. Some of us bedded down there.

I decided to sleep in the warehouse beside the old fur press. I wanted to be alone there to catch, perhaps, the feeling of the days when Duck Lake Post was alive. It was dark when I went over, and the great door complained when I put my shoulder against it and pushed it in. I lit a stub of a candle and placed it on a shelf, laid out my bag in the center and close to the open door, lay there in the flickering candlelight surveying my abode. To one side was a beaten-up freighter canoe long unused, on the other the press, a huge one with a great screw turned by an iron bar. Into that press had gone the fur to be made up into bales for the trip down the Wolverine to South Indian, or down the Seal to the Bay. Along the walls were shelves for storage, and rows of hooks for hides. I could see it in the spring after the fur was in, foxes and wolves, muskrats and beaver, wolverine, mink, and otter. I could smell it, too, for even though the hides were long gone, their pungence remained, an almost fetid and musky smell, a combination of all the creatures trapped in the north. Here, years before, lay the wealth of the region, the result of un-counted days and months of labor, privation, and danger. It had once held food and traps and equipment for all the sur-rounding native bands. This was more than a warehouse for fur and supplies, it was a bastion of security for all who lived within range.

I blew out the candle finally and went to sleep. Not a sound disturbed me all night long; no howling of huskies, no scurry-ing of mice or squirrels. I wakened once and listened, but there was only the lap of the waves down at the shore. The night was cloudy and dark and though I had braced the door with a stout log, it creaked in the rising wind.

In the morning to my joy the sun was out and I went onto the ramp to dress and to lace my boots. The planks were hand-hewn, shaped with axe and knife and rasp and held to-gether with wooden dowel pins. That approach to the great door was made to last. Up it had come bales and boxes from the canoes and boats and sleds, and down had gone the pressed bales of fur. I threw on my parka, went down to the shore and washed in the icy water, then walked down the length of the peninsula. The stakes that marked the tents were still in place and, with them, the debris of all Indian camps, shreds of cloth, worn moccasins, torn rubbers, the whitened, well-gnawed bones of caribou.

It seemed to me I could almost hear the Indians talking, could smell their fires, sense the coming and going. The country itself was the same. The barren tundra stretched endlessly in all directions, and marching up the hills were the scattered spruce of the Taiga in which the caribou sought shelter from winter storms. The lake sparkled in the sunshine as it had for thousands of years, the land itself as beautiful and full of meaning and challenge as it had ever been. Something was gone, however, a certain something that had been there before. It was Duck Lake Post that had changed with its abandonment.

I stood at the far end of the spit looking back toward the post with its rising plume of smoke, picturing it as it used to be when the smoke of many fires hung like a haze over the entire point. Greetings, goodbyes, tales of high adventure, sadness, and joy—all these were gone.

I knew then that though one loves a land, one still needs the warmth of companionship with others of his kind and must not always travel alone. This was the truth, for I had ghost camps of my own and country haunted with memories of those who had been with me. One of these places was a little campsite at the mouth of the Range River where it empties into Low Lake in the Quetico-Superior country. No one but my partner and I had ever used this spot, for from the water's edge it looked like a marshy flat; but actually beyond the fringe of alders it was high and dry, with the shelf of grass sheltered well by a broadly branching jackpine. Here we laid our sleeping bags and gear when the bluebill flight was on, and for many years knew such companionship as only those can who share some common joy.

The place for the fire was close to a shelf of gray rock in back of the pine, and at night, if we had any luck, the light shone on the blue and green of wingbars, and the branches of the jackpine were a tracery of black above us. We stored our food in a crevice of the rock and always tucked away some kindling for a quick fire there. The river wound behind us, an open road to the Range Lake country and the border, while to the south and west were the golden rice beds, with a stand of tall pines against the sunsets. The decoys were placed in the mouth of the river for sooner or later something always came by. I will never forget the breath-taking roar of a bunch of bluebills coming down the river, the canvas-ripping sound of them as they dipped. Sometimes mallards lifted out of the rice and headed up river. Jacksnipe always began the day with their cheeping, and after dawn flocks of snowbirds drifted across the mud flats bordering the channel.

For many years Dean and I used the place and we came to love its sights and sounds and smells and the joy of all these things together, but then one day he took the trail to another hunting ground and our joy was gone. For a while I went back alone as though he were still with me and I could hear his banter, then, and see him moving around as he used to do. When I lay in my sleeping bag on the grassy shelf, I was conscious of the depression beside me, and when a flock came over high, I could hear him whisper, "Listen—there'll be action in the morning."

After a time I no longer returned to my ghost camp. It was better, I thought, to keep it with memories that were mine alone. For me that little camp had become a place of dreams. Others may go there now and perhaps they are finding what I found and building associations of their own. And so it is with all country. While the meaning of wilderness never changes to those who understand it, it means even more if you have sunk your roots in deeply. No country can ever be bleak or forbidding if it has once been a part of the love and warmth of those who have shared it with you.

Whenever I travel the lake and river country of the north, I meet friends of other days. They are with me constantly on the campsites and I meet them on portages, and hear them everywhere. Never again will I travel the Rainy, the Churchill, the Camsell, the Bear, or the Burntwood, or any other routes without reliving adventures with companions who have been with me.

The terrain has a different meaning now, not only through what we shared, but because of what we had known that gave us the feeling of the land itself, its eras of the past, the time when the Canadian Shield came into being, when prehistoric seas laid down formations of Athabasca sandstone, the glacial periods of the last million years when the routes we traveled were shaped by the gouging of the ice, the crossing of Asiatics over Bering Strait and their slow filtration into the south, the days of explorers and *voyageurs*, up to the swiftly changing time of today. All this we had shared and lived over many thousands of miles until almost unconsciously the long history of the primitive country we had traversed was absorbed into our minds and thoughts. We had left no mark on the country itself, but the land had left its mark on us.

The smoke was still rising high from the kitchen of the old post. Breakfast must be ready and I hurried back. The wind was coming up and we still had far to go.

CHAPTER XII

FOND DU LAC

Fond du lac means the end of a waterway, a *voyageur*'s term, usually a place where a river flows in or out of a lake. I know a Fond du lac on Lake Superior where the St. Louis empties into waters from the north; another on Lake Winnebago in Wisconsin; a third far to the northwest between Lake Athabasca and the Wollaston, a river that should have been a major fur-trading route but, because of many rapids and shallows, was never popular. David Thompson, the great map-maker (Mr. Astronomer Thompson, as he was known to the Northwest and to the Hudson's Bay Companies), dreamed of using it as a short cut to far-off Fort Chipewyan where Athabasca meets the Slave on its way to the Mackenzie, but this was not to be. His exploration in 1796 was fraught with so many misadventures that only one official expedition followed—when J. B. Tyrrell of the Canadian Geological Survey traveled the route a century later.

The records of the past century therefore shed scant light on what the river was like. When little is known about an area, legendry and imagination have a habit of filling in the gaps. So it was with the Fond du lac we proposed to follow from the height of land west of Reindeer and Wollaston to the head of Lake Athabasca.

As we prepared to leave Winnipeg, we heard the first of these stories from an old-timer who claimed to have been close to the country during his prospecting and trapping days.

"The rapids up there are terrible," he told us, "no, they're worse than that, absolutely horrible, and no canoes can run them. The portages were given up so long ago, there isn't a trace of them anywhere; no choice but to shoot—or hack your way through."

Another said: "I have heard the Fond du lac is bad to travel, but the flies are what get a man down. There is no place in the whole north including the tundra, where they're as bad— black flies, bull dogs, deer flies, mosquitoes. They're really something and I've seen them pretty rough."

We had excellent aerial surveys, and while few white men had actually been on the ground, our maps were reliable and made us wonder at the authenticity of all legends, especially one—more fantastic than the rest—that had the Fond du lac disappearing into the ground.

"There's one place on that river," an Indian is supposed to have said, "where it goes down into a big hole. None of our people ever go there. It is a spirit place where a Manito lives."

When we reached the end of Wollaston, some ninety miles of open lake with island mirages lying everywhere, we were somewhat curious and not a little apprehensive. Surely, we thought, there must be some basis for these tales, some good reason why no Indians lived there any more. The outlet bay was very pronounced and as we approached there was evidence of flow into the mouth of the river. We were totally unprepared, however, for our first view of the Fond du lac. The bay narrowed sharply and, as we neared, we saw thousands of huge boulders like a wall across the opening of the river. The closer we came, the thicker grew the rocks; and we could see nothing but a great unbroken field of them, with pools of water in between.

We paddled along the edge, but nowhere was space wide enough to take a canoe. If this were the mouth of the Fond du lac, it was almost dry; and if this first rapids were typical, we would have rough going indeed. I climbed out on one of the larger rocks and looked down the river. As far as the first bend, there was no open water in sight but, where the river began to swing, there seemed to be a lead. We might traverse the boulder field, but what lay ahead? Was that sliver of blue water ahead continuous, or were the channels dry? Would we have to portage for miles down a dry stream bed, spend several weeks of back-breaking work instead of one in covering the one-hundred-and-fifty-odd miles to Stony Rapids

Post? Perhaps the dour predictions we had heard were not fantasy after all. If the beginning were an indication of what the rest would be, the best thing to do was retrace our steps, go back to Reindeer the way we had come. No party relishes retracing a route and admitting defeat, and never in our experience had we been forced to do so. We all decided to cross the boulders, see what it was like beyond, and if there were any chance at all, to go on if it took until freezeup.

We tried separate channels through the boulders, probed and retreated, dragged the canoes over the rocks, only to return, eventually deciding there was no way but to portage. Between the boulders was water from two to six feet deep, but none of it continuous. In desperation, we unloaded, shouldered the packs, and began jumping from rock to rock. Many of them were slippery and we fell between, but finally the whole outfit was across and piled up safely close to the lead of the open water which, to our joy, seemed to go beyond the bend. Now came the canoes, an entirely different matter. Carrying one on a portage trail is simple, but getting from boulder to boulder is something else. All the time I kept thinking, "if this kind of portaging is ahead, what will happen to the canoes, our outfit, to legs and ankles, should we slip and fall with heavy loads?"

After a couple of hours the canoes were also across and loaded. There was no question anymore of returning and going back down the Blondeau, the Swan, and Reindeer's hundred mile stretch to the south. We were now determined to go on and take whatever came.

We ran two small rapids in succession on our way to Hatchet Lake. They, too, were full of boulders but at least there were channels of deep water and we had no difficulty. David Thompson, in coming up stream from Black Lake, must have been just as happy at finding the river in good flow, for he said in his diary:

"The River had now increased it's water by the addition of the Porcupine and Trout Rivers, and several Brooks; it had also a greater descent; In it's course of One hundred and fifty three miles from the above place of observation in the Black Lake, it meets with and forms many small Lakes; and collects their waters to form a stream of about one, to two, hundred yards in width; it's bottom is sand and pebbles, or rude stones and small rocks, smoothed by the water; on a bed of Limestone, which is the rock of the country; its course is sinuous, from the many hills it meets, and runs around in it's passage; its current is strong, with many rapids, some of them a mile in length: it has four falls. Three of these are about half way down the River; the fourth fall is at the end of a series of rapids, cutting through a high hill; at length the banks become perpendicular, and the river falls eight feet, the carrying place is six hundred yards in length."

We came to know the Fond du lac's rapids and enjoyed them, for none was impassable, the boulders cushioned by enough water so that when we hurtled toward them we rode the swirl and were carried past without touching. We felt as we had on the Sturgeon Weir when leaving the Churchill far to the south, a sense of slaloming as a skier does, sweeping from one stretch of white water to another with the assurance there was always a way through. We portaged around the falls but ran most of the fast water. So confident did we become that, rather than worry about rocks, we watched for grayling leaping ahead of the canoes. Whenever they seemed particularly active, we landed below, broke out the fly rods and began to cast.

I have seen many grayling but never any so completely exciting in their taking of a fly. It may have been the fact they were really hungry, but they rose clear of the water, sometimes several feet, to take the fly on the way down. As soon as the nose of a fish was close, a twitch of the rod tip and it was on. Almost every cast brought a fish, beautiful ones in those clear, cold waters, sixteen to twenty inches in length, weighing up to two-and-a-half pounds, their chief glory the great iridescent dorsal fin with its bright orange border. We kept only enough for a meal ahead, lost track of how many were landed and released. Once, watching a grayling, we narrowly missed a sharp ledge and disaster.

We now knew Thompson's diary by heart and, with the river completely navigable, no longer had any fear. Rapids after rapids disappeared behind us and, where there was any doubt, we waded the shallows and lined the canoes down rather than portage. We had left that great outpouring of granite, schist, and basalt that is known all over the north as the Canadian Shield and were now traveling through a sedimentary formation of limestone. The banks had been carved into caves, canyons, and strangely sculptured battlements where the soft and relatively soluble ledges had been subject to the erosion of the river.

Coming around a sharp bend where the water was very fast, we were watching a particularly interesting cavern. The canoe was moving swiftly, no more than twenty feet from shore. Suddenly, out of the cave stepped a magnificent wolf. It was yellowish white with a distinct ruff of black over its shoulders. For a long moment it stood there, as though aware of the tableau it made, then loped off leisurely along the bank onto a sandspit and was lost to sight. We landed just beyond, and there were its tracks leading across and toward the south. Patches of crowberry and signs of feeding ravens were everywhere, their droppings splashes of purple on rocks and driftwood.

The wolf was the first we had seen on the trip and I was thrilled, for more than any other animal in the north, it is the epitome of wilderness. I can still see its smooth loose-jointed movement, almost a flowing of muscle and sinew.

One night we camped on a high ledge of limestone from which we had a view of the river for miles to the west. So steep was the approach, we were forced to get our water by dropping a bucket on a line into the river. Such a campsite one dreams about, a rushing river below, a view into the sunset, tremendous rock formations on either side. If this, I thought, should ever become a national park, the scene might become world famous. Not as spectacular as Yellowstone, Yosemite, or Jasper, it had a wild, untouched beauty and character of its own. To think we were some of the few who had actually seen it in over a century of time!

The west reddened and, as we sat there in the glow, a moose came out from shore half a mile away; a bull with a great spread of antlers, it walked majestically into the shallows and began wading across, slashing the color as it advanced. On a long sand bar in the very center of the river it stopped, head held high, then splashed through the sunset glow until it disappeared in the timber of the opposite bank.

The following day we passed the place where David Thompson came to grief. After many rapids and stretches of fast water, so many we lost count, the river dropped over a series of ledges impossible to run or avoid. We landed well above, looked for a portage and found it on the left side, a trail that skirted a clump of birches close to the water's edge. Here the great map-maker almost lost his life.

"On our return," he states in his diary, "and about half way up the black river [the Fond du lac], we came to one of the falls, with a strong rapid both above and below it, we had a carrying place of 200 yards, we then attempted the strong current above the fall, they were to track the canoe up by a line, walking on shore, while I steered it, when they had proceeded about eighty yards, they came to a birch tree, growing at the edge of the water, and there stood and disputed between themselves on which side of the tree the tracking line should pass. I called to them to go on, they could not hear me for the noise of the fall, I then waved my hand for them to proceed, meanwhile the current was drifting me out, and having only one hand to guide the canoe, the Indians standing still, the canoe took a sheer across the current, to prevent the canoe upsetting, I waved my hand to them to let go the line and leave me to my fate, which they obeyed. I sprang to the bow of the canoe took out my clasp knife, cut the line from the canoe and put the knife in my pocket, by this time I was on the head of the fall, all I could do was to place the canoe to go down bow foremost, in an instant the canoe was precipitated down the fall and buried under the waves, I was struck out of the canoe and when I arose among the waves, the canoe came on me and buried beneath it, to raise myself I struck my feet against the rough bottom and came up close to the canoe which I grasped and being now in shoal water, I was able to conduct the canoe to the shore."

According to his diary he lost almost everything:

"nothing remained in the canoe but an ax, a small tent of grey cotton, and my gun: also a pewter basin. When the canoe was hauled on shore I had to lay down on the rocks, wounded, bruised, and exhausted by my exertions."

The Indians had run down along the shore and returned with the precious cork-lined box containing his sextant and a few instruments, the papers of his survey, and maps. All Thompson had left was his shirt and a thin, linen vest. His companions had also lost everything they owned, so for protection and warmth they cut the tent into three pieces to wrap around themselves as a defense against flies and the cold at night.

As Thompson rose from the rocks where he lay, he found blood on his left foot and saw that the flesh, from the heel almost to the toes, had been torn away when he struck his feet against the bottom. The Indians bound his foot with part of the tent, and helped him to stand. Unassisted he walked over the carrying place with its "rude stones and banks."

The Indians went into the woods to find gum to patch the badly broken canoe, but they were confronted with the problem of starting a fire because they had lost their firesteel and flint. Thompson took the flint from the one remaining gun and when he drew out his knife from his pocket, to use the steel, he said it was "as though I had drawn a ghost out of my pocket and I heard them whisper to each other, how avaricious a white man must be, who rushing on death takes care of his little knife."

"I said to them, if I had not saved my little knife, how could we make a fire, you fools go to the Birch Trees and get some touch wood which they soon brought, a fire was made, we repaired our canoe and carried all above the Fall and the Rapid, they carried the canoe, my share was the gun, axe, and pewter basin; and Sextant Box. Late in the evening we made a fire and warmed ourselves. It was now our destitute condition that stared us in the face, a long journey through barren country, without provisions or the means of obtaining any, almost naked, and suffering from the weather, all before us was very dark, but I had hopes that the Supreme Being through our Great Redeemer to whom I made short prayers morning and evening would find some way to preserve us; on the second day, in the afternoon we came on a small lake of the river and in a grassy bay we saw two large Gulls hovering, this lead us to think they were taking care of their young, we went and found three young gulls, which we put in the canoe, it may be remarked the Gull cannot dive, he is too light; these gulls gave us but little meat. They had not four ounces of meat on them. It appeared to sharpen hunger."

The next day they found an eagle's nest some sixteen feet above the ground in the spreading branches of a birch tree. The Indian, Kozdah, was sent to rob the nest, but in the midst of his depredations, the old ones arrived and Thompson and the other Indian pelted them with stones and shouted until the young were thrown out of the nest onto the ground. Kozdah picked up one of them, but the young bird drove its talons so deeply into his wrist, Thompson was forced to cut the foot from the body before it was released.

They cleaned and roasted the birds and during the night awoke in the throes of violent dysentery. Thompson made a strong brew of Labrador tea which helped them recover. Day after day from then on they lived on crowberries, which are not nutritious and sometimes even poisonous, until, as Thompson said, "Both Paddy [the other Indian] and myself were now like skeletons, effects of hunger, dysentery, from cold nights, and so weak, that we thought it useless to go any further but die where we were."

Kozdah was in much better shape than his companions for

he had known the danger of eating the fat of young eagles, had therefore avoided the entrails and had escaped the aftermath of dysentery. His conscience began to bother him for not warning the others and he was concerned for fear they might perish and he be blamed. Neither Thompson nor Paddy suspected the truth when Kozdah's morale began to weaken.

"Kozdah," wrote Thompson, "now burst into tears, upon which we told him that he was yet strong as he had not suffered from the disease. He replied, if both of you die, I am sure to be killed for everyone will believe I have killed you both, the white men will revenge your death on me and the Indians will do the same for him; I told him then to get some thin white birch rind, and I would give him a writing, when he did, with charcoal, I then wrote a short account of our situation, which I gave him upon which he said now I am safe."

Finally the starving and desperate men met with a party of Chipewyans who gave them food, flint and steel, a pair of shoes, and a kettle, after which Thompson wrote:

"We now proceeded on our journey with thanks to God and cheerful hearts and without any accident on the 21st of July arrived at Fairford House from whence we commenced our journey. From this time to the 26th of August, our time was spent in fishing and hunting, and with all our exertions could barely maintain ourselves."

As we sat on our campsite that night listening to the roar

of the river below, Thompson was very much with us. Though he had been there over a century and a half before, it could have happened yesterday, so little had the country changed. During the day we had seen several eagles, as well as gulls and ducks, but outside of the wolf, the moose, and one caribou several days back, had seen no game. We were on the Fond du lac almost a month later than Thompson which accounted for the lack of flies, and he was coming upstream when he wrote his account, while we were going down.

What interested me most in his diary was how the character of the great map-maker emerged during his time of crisis. Why he told Kozdah and Paddy to cast him loose and then cut his tracking line, I do not know, but taking the time while plunging over the falls to place his knife back into his pocket was typical of the man. In the face of death, he did the customary, routine thing. His was a mind that brooked no deviation, and he showed here the indomitable will and courage that had carried him all over the northwest.

When we approached Manito Falls, we realized it must be the place where the river was supposed to disappear. From both Thompson's and Tyrrell's accounts we knew it could be no other, and that unless some recent geological catastrophe had taken place, there was nothing to the story we had heard. Nevertheless, we were curious, knowing from past experience that there must be some basis for such a legend. As we neared, the river narrowed, the banks grew more precipitous, and we could hear a roar ahead and see spray and mist over the trees. Rounding a bend, we saw a quarter of a mile away the hole through which the river supposedly plunged.

This evidently was the turning point beyond which Indians would not go. We beached the canoes and climbed the bank; from there it seemed as though the river actually did go down into a gigantic opening. We studied the spot and quickly found the reason. At this place the river made a sharp, almost right-angled turn, so sharp that even from a height it could not be seen to continue. The rocks on either side were deeply eroded and, from where we stood, it looked as though the river went down between the banks. Into the canoes once more, we approached warily. The current grew stronger. We hugged the shore. Just before the bend, we landed on a flat shelf and climbed a ridge. From a high rock we could see the river beyond. It did not disappear!—it was merely lost to view as it plunged between the steep limestone walls of what had looked like a cavern.

Thompson described it graphically:

"For half a mile further the current is very swift; it is then for one hundred and eighteen yards, compressed in a narrow channel of rock only twelve yards in width. At the end of this channel a bold perpendicular-sided point of limestone rock projects at right angles to the course of the river, against which the rapid current rushes and appears driven back with such force that the whole river seems as if turned up from its bottom. It boils, foams and every drop is white; part of the water is driven down a precipice of twenty feet descent; the greater part rushes through the point of rock and disappears for two hundred yards; then issues out in boiling whirlpools. The dashing of the water against the rocks, the deep roar of the torrent, the hollow sound of the fall, with the surrounding high, frowning hills form a scenery grand and awful, and it is well named the Manito Fall. While the Nahathaways possessed the country, they made offerings to it, and thought it the residence of a Manito; they have retired to milder climates; and the Chipewyans have taken their place who make no offerings to anything; but my companions were so awe struck, that the one gave a ring, and the other a bit of tobacco. They heard of this Fall, but never saw it before."

It was midafternoon so decided to pitch our camp near the falls. We found a good place for the tents back from the water's edge, and a cooking spot on a flat ledge in full view of the river's awesome drop into the gorge below. A sea gull sat quietly on a point of rock to one side of the falls. Every so often it would take off to circle the swirl below, usually picking up a small fish before returning to its perch. Time and again it did this, merely spreading its wings and floating down below to search the foam-laced whirlpools. No doubt some gull had sat there when Thompson with his two companions Paddy and Kozdah came through.

After camp was pitched and supper out of the way, we walked around and surveyed our site. Growing over the rocks was a finely leaved heather I had not seen before, possibly a sub-arctic species of Labrador tea. The flowers were gone, but color was beginning to show everywhere. Most of the evening we sat and looked at the falls and listened to its roar, and that night went to sleep with the air full of its thunder.

In the morning we made the portage and pushed down the current. As we rounded the first bend, the sound of Manito Falls was gone and with it the legend of the river that disappeared and all the fearsome stories we had heard. If legends are runes, we had run them down; if runes are truths, feelings, and mysteries, we had found them on the Fond du lac, but more than that was our sense of having traveled with a great explorer, Mr. Astronomer Thompson, and of having known the joys and hazards that were his on this forgotten and seldom-used route of the past.

CHAPTER XIII

SPELL OF THE YUKON

I DID NOT reach the Yukon until a few years ago, but long before that my vision of it was a vivid one, painted by that master of far-north balladry, Robert Service. Somehow in spite of grandiloquent language, a highly romantic interpretation of the land of the famous gold strike of ninety-eight, his ballads caught something nebulous that no one else quite achieved, a quality that even today over half a century later enthralls those who know the bush and the life of the frontiers.

Ever since that memorable day of my boyhood when I discovered him, the Yukon meant something special to me.

The very sound of the name had magic, a land of wild, primitive beauty where men made fortunes in gold or lost all they had, where they struggled and died against impossible odds. Born too late to take part in the great adventure, I was thrilled by the tales that came out of those fabulous years. Though I had talked to men who had been there, fondled their nuggets, listened in awe and envy as they told what they had done, it was Robert Service who made the Yukon come alive for me; and I can quote him yet with as much feeling as when I first ran across his booklet of gold-rush ballads.

> *There's a whisper on the night wind, there's a*
> *star agleam to guide us,*
> *And the wild is calling, calling . . . let us go.*

There was the essence of my feeling for the Yukon. I lived with the words "And the wild is calling, calling—let us go" until the far reaches of the north became an obsession with me and at times I was filled with unbearable longing for a land I had never known. When I could stand it no longer, I often took my dog-eared volume and read aloud the lines that gripped me most.

> *Have you gazed on naked grandeur where there's*
> *nothing else to gaze on?*
> *In the hush of mountained fastness, in the flush*
> *of midnight skies.*
> *I am the land that listens, I am the land that broods.*

The pictures those words painted of the Yukon stayed with me. Though I have seen much wild country in my roamings since those early impressionable years, because of Service, the Yukon stood apart and alone and for me assumed the stature of a haunting legend. Several times in my travels I came close to its borders and once even glimpsed its shining peaks from the Mackenzie River's Mount Charles, below Fort Norman. As I sat there that day, high above the valley and looked off to the west, the old thrill was still there and I knew before long I must make my sentimental journey to the fields of gold and romance.

When I finally did reach the Yukon, I had seen too much to expect it to be the land I had imagined. I knew however, that somewhere away from roads and towns, and airplanes, I would find what Service had written about. My expedition would in a sense be a search for a long lost boyhood dream.

I landed at historic Skagway, once the roughest and most notorious camp in the world, the port which was the jumping-off place for the gold rush. Here was where the ships put in, coming north from Seattle and San Francisco. Skagway had actually changed little, the vistas of glistening ice fields, the towering mountains seen from the Lynn Canal were the same, the beach and the flat where once thousands of tents were pitched, with equipment and supplies strewn helter-skelter from end to end, the main street with its false-fronted buildings, the terrible trail itself leading from the flat and winding up through the pass. I walked up and down

Broadway and imagined how it had been in 1898, but some-how it seemed unreal, a sort of movie backdrop with a worn-out facade of the past.

True, this is where it all began and I could see the route go-ing up through the gorge, the desperate forty-five miles that had tried men's souls. I did not make the climb as they did, but rode over it on a narrow-gauge railway, the White Pass and Yukon, built to transport men and supplies to the head of navigation above the Yukon River.

In places, from the train windows, the trail could still be seen and I pictured the long line of men packing their outfits up that killing slope in waist deep snow, sensed their desper-ate hurry and confusion. As the train clattered on. I remem-bered the beaten and starving mules and horses, the stench of rotting flesh in Dead Horse Gulch—once filled with so many carcasses, the trail led over them. But recapturing the scene from a comfortable seat on a train was impossible. That was another age, and the lines of Service seemed without mean-ing or authenticity.

Never was seen such an army, pitiful, futile, unfit,
Never was seen such a spirit, manifold courage and grit.

When the train climbed up over the divide, I stood on the platform and felt the icy winds sweeping across the smooth glaciated surfaces of the plateau. Many, I knew, had turned back there rather than continue to the water of Lake Bennett.

Before me was the bay where ten thousand men once camped while building boats and scows for their trip down the river to the gold fields. An old weather-beaten church still stood; on top of the rise a few tumble-down cabins were scattered along the slope; beyond was nothing but brush and scrubby trees, clear across the valley.

"Isn't it exciting," said someone beside me, "just imagine what took place here."

I looked at a faded photograph of the sea of tents, the black clots of men, but somehow it still seemed unreal.

I am the land that listens, I am the land that broods.

We stopped for lunch at Bennett. It was served mining camp style on long tables to give the atmosphere of the days of ninety-eight. The food was good and plentiful, but I was glad when we moved on. This was interesting and I enjoyed seeing the old places I had read about, but nowhere yet was the feeling of that elusive something I had come to find.

At White Horse that night, a bustling frontier town with dusty streets, grinding trucks, a thirteen-million-dollar airport, and a sort of bursting-at-the-seams vitality, I found a quiet eating place down near the old Yukon River waterfront. The restaurant dated back proudly to the good old days and had not changed much in sixty years. The walls were covered with pictures, maps and mementos. Not far away was the landing, and after dinner I walked over there to look at the Yukon steamers now up on dry land, the remnants of a fleet of once-proud river boats, scroll work on their bridges and, along their sides, tall stacks and enormous paddle wheels. They were the type that plied the Mississippi long after the Civil War, the *Showboat*, the *Robert E. Lee*, the *Henry Clay*. These had different names, *Klondike*, *Dawson City*, *Casca*, *Tagish*, but were much the same—wood burners made to navigate a river with sand bars, rapids, and sharp bends. Now they sat waiting to be dismantled. Only one would be kept as a museum and for an occasional trip down river. It was now being rebuilt, smoke was coming out of its stacks, and on shore a pile of cordwood waited to be loaded.

As I stood there, I thought of the thousands who had ridden those boats to Dawson City at the mouth of the Klondike, men full of dreams and hopes, how some had stayed while others returned, broken and lost, or with fortunes that stirred uncounted others to come and try their luck. I thought of the heartbreak, suffering, and starvation of these men who, unprepared—and many just off city streets—had suddenly come face to face with an untamed, rugged land, with brutality, hunger and greed, of the frenzy with which they streamed from the gold hungry states to the frozen north with the cry: "Gold—Gold in the Klondike—On to the Yukon," until it seemed as though they had been seized with madness.

Still I felt there must be something more that drove many of them on, something more impelling than the lure of the gold itself or the chance of making a fortune—the fierce wild beauty of the land and the test in pitting their strength against it, the comradeship in sharing hardship, disaster, and triumph, the vast and utter loneliness, the joyous song of a creek tumbling down a mountain side, the feel of spring after the stark and bitter cold of a long winter. This was the backdrop to the search for gold and when Service wrote: "Men of the High North, the wild sky is blazing," he was thinking of all this, and deep down in his heart, in all the strange tales he wove into his ballads, was the feeling of men for the north.

The following morning I went over to Miles Canyon above White Horse. A dam had been built at the foot of the rapids, so it was no longer the raging flood it had been. I studied the river where so many had come to grief, where food, supplies, and equipment that had been packed over the White Pass was lost forever. From the rocky banks of the gorge, I tried to see it as it used to be, the surge of white horses and the high crest in the center, the treacherous cliffs and rocks on either side and at its base. As a canoeman with many rapids behind me, I could understand why that stretch of river had thrown fear into all and why lives had been lost there.

It was while standing below Miles Canyon that I first began to get an intimation of the feeling I had been searching for. Picturing the old swirls and danger spots described so vividly in the diaries, it seemed I could see above me the waiting men who, having battled their way over the trail, were now ready to make the last supreme effort to reach their goal. To these Cheechakos, the name given to tenderfeet, it was a matter of life and death. This rapids would settle the score.

Shooting the wrath of my rapids, scaling my ramparts of snow.

Service had caught it all, the fear of men hurtling down that wild canyon in boats and scows, men who knew nothing of white water, I could see the ungainly craft yaw and swing in the cross currents and whirlpools, then crack up against the rocks. Forgotten at the moment was the train ride up and over the pass from Skagway, the lunch at Lake Bennett, the remains of old mining camps. This seemed real at last.

But it was not until I made a trip into the country south and west of the Yukon with my son Sig and with Joe Langevin, a game warden, that I came to the end of my quest. We were in the Kluane Game Sanctuary and had climbed to a broad and open plateau.

"Here," said Joe, "is sheep country, we'll sit here a while and look over the skyline."

Around us were snow-covered ranges and peaks. We were in a great amphitheater and had grandstand seats. The warden had a spotting scope and field glasses and was studying the ridges intently.

"There they are," he said finally, "about thirty."

He handed me the glasses and I saw them at once, a cluster of white dots against the brown tundra-covered hillsides. But through the spotting scope those little dots became ewes and rams, almost, it seemed, within a stone's throw. They were feeding and resting undisturbed for we were too far away for them to hear us or get our scent. One great ram stood on an outcrop away from the rest. He did not feed, simply stood there and watched.

"Dall sheep," said Joe, "this is one of the best places for them in the whole Yukon."

Within a couple of hours we had spotted 191 sheep in small, scattered groups on the slopes around us. Some were near, within half a mile, but most were at least twice that far.

I left my companions after a time and walked toward one of the groups, crossed a low ridge, and was alone. It was as though I had walked through an open door and closed it quietly behind me. Then I became aware of the immensity of the scene and the silence. Below lay a bank of ice and snow, brown and discolored for the wind had blown its dust upon it. A ground squirrel chittered at me from its burrow to one side. Small brown birds that looked like siskins twittered and flew around the ice, feeding on the seeds of grasses and flowers which had bloomed there a month before. The twittering in that all engulfing quiet was almost loud. Never before had those tiny flute-like notes seemed so distinct and clear. The sheep paid no attention to me, worked their way up and down the hills as though I were not there.

I've stood in some mighty mouthed hollow
That's plumb full of hush to the brim.

Here was the hush; a sense of enormous and almost crush-ing silence lay over the land. This was the old Yukon at last.

In the afternoon we went up to Bullion Creek to see a placer operation there, crossed and crisscrossed the stream with its braided channels and shifting gravel bars, finally came to a power shovel with a drag line, a bulldozer and a sluice. A two-man operation, it was small compared to some of the great dredges working out of Fairbanks. We heard the machines long before we saw them, a yellow monster of clanking noise and steel squatting in the middle of the stream chewing its way into the gold-bearing gravel, a bulldozer push-ing the dirt into a sluice which disgorged the worthless rock and kept the gold. In an hour's time, this combination could do more work than a lone prospector could do in many days. The outfit cost a great deal of money but in a good season might sluice out fifty thousand dollars worth of gold. Each time the clean-up came and the final washing was done, a small fortune was made, but the work was hard, dangerous and dirty, and the men who tended their behemoths seldom slept—for the season was short. The lure of gold and the hardship was there.

With such equipment, the whole bottom of a creek could be dug out and sluiced. Nothing was missed and, when the monsters were through, the bed of a stream looked as though it had been gouged by a glacier; only a vast and tumbled mass of moraine remained.

> *Ripping the guts of my mountains, looting the beds of my creeks.*

The search was going on as of old, with the same desperate violence, the same struggle, but back in ninety-eight, it was more of a personal thing, man against nature with only his own strength and courage to sustain him. This was finding gold too, but it wasn't like wading into a creek, panning the gravel and sand, and seeing the color there.

So we picked up shovels and pans from one of the cabins, went down to a place where it looked as though the creek bottom had not been disturbed. I dug out a shovelful of dirt close to the bed rock, dumped it into my pan, dipped up some water and began to slosh it gently with a circular motion, washing clay and larger particles of rock out over the rim. After a time I added more water and again got rid of what I did not want. Gradually the water cleared, with only black sand remaining. This was pay dirt and I continued very carefully until there was nothing more to come out. At the end only a spoonful remained and this I held to the light.

Color! A thin flake of gold no more than an eighth of an inch in size was in the pan. It was clean and yellow and I looked at it with delight, picked it up and dropped it carefully into a small bottle. Another shovelful of dirt and I began again, ending up as before, with a tiny residue. Beside the sand were several small grains, miniature nuggets exactly like the big ones, except for size. Those yellow grains of gold were what led men up the little nameless creeks, watching, always watching for color as they searched and panned every likely looking prospect.

"A hard working miner could make a grubstake here," said Joe, "and possibly a little more beside."

We kept on and were oblivious of time. The creek gurgled merrily by and as I looked into it I saw the black ledges of volcanic rock at its base. Against that rock and in its fissures and crevices were nuggets and flakes of gold settled-out over many centuries. Heavier than the other components of the stream bed, these fragments from some mother lode above had been washed out of the grand matrix in ten thousand or a million springs. The bed of the creek itself was a long sluice box, the flood waters doing the work over and over again, the gold always sinking to the bottom. It was simply dredging on a gigantic scale.

I left my panning finally and turned over a few boulders, examining them carefully underneath. Where they had lain against the clay might be a few flakes or even a nugget or two if the boulder had not been moved. Though I searched carefully, I found nothing.

"All this stuff must have come from upstream," said Sig, as he carefully screened the last sand from his panning, "this didn't just happen."

Joe laughed, "That's what always got 'em," he said, "any man who has ever seen color in his pan has looked upstream and wondered."

I knew the prospectors had swarmed over every tributary of the Yukon and the Klondike for hundreds of miles in all directions from Dawson City at its mouth. Not a chance had been overlooked in the frantic quest. They left their diggings almost before they began, worked upstream—staking out claims as they went—in the hope of finding the mother lode and a bonanza. An old prospector still working a claim on the Klondike put it well.

"This country," he said, "is too big to know all of it. In the early days, they were in a hurry and couldn't possibly have covered every chance. Why," he exclaimed, and I could see the old gleam in his eyes, "there's big stretches no one has ever been in."

> *For once you've panned the speckled sand and seen the*
>   *bonny dust,*
> *Its peerless brightness blinds you like a spell.*
> *It's little else you care about; you go because you must,*
> *And you feel that you could follow it to hell.*

This was the Yukon men talked about, the lure of gold that brought so many thousands to the far north. In the little panning I had done, I had caught just a hint of what the old-time prospectors had known. But the part of the Yukon they seldom mentioned was the irresistable spell of a vast and lonely land, its enormous silences, its challenge, and primeval power. The land had changed, it was true, but its elusive spell was still there. Even those who returned to civilization, long after they had forgotten the gold and spent the riches they had found, remembered that while they were in the Yukon their lives had been washed with color.

"Once you've known the bush, you're never the same," is an old adage in the north. While the reason for coming was gold, it was the bush that changed men's lives. The spell of the Yukon was compounded of so many things no man could ever define it. Even Service failed, but in the line "And the Wild is calling—calling," he caught something, and all who have known the country understand what he was trying to say. He touched a responsive chord in the hearts and minds of millions of men.

FROM

THE SINGING
WILDERNESS

CHAPTER XIV

CAMPFIRES

Sᴏᴍᴇᴛʜɪɴɢ happens to a man when he sits before a fire. Strange stirrings take place within him, and a light comes into his eyes which was not there before. An open flame suddenly changes his environment to one of adventure and romance. Even an indoor fireplace has this effect, though its owner is protected by four walls and the assurance that, should the fire go out, his thermostat will keep him warm. No matter where an open fire happens to be, in a city apartment, a primitive cabin, or deep in the wilderness, it weaves its spell.

Before men ever dreamed of shelter, campfires were their homes. Here they gathered and made their first plans for communal living, for tribal hunts and raids. Here for centuries they dreamed vague dreams and became slowly aware of the first faint glimmerings and nebulous urges that eventually were to widen the gulf between them and the primitive darkness from which they sprang.

Although the gulf is wide, even now we see the future in leaping flames, making plans in their enchantment which in the brash light of day seem foolhardy. Before them, modern conquests are broached and unwritten pledges made which vary little from those of the past. Around a fire men feel that the whole world is their campsite and all men partners of the trail.

Once a man has known the warmth and companionship there, once he has tasted the thrill of stories of the chase with the firelight in his eyes, he has made contact with the past, recaptured some of the lost wonder of his early years and some of the sense of mystery of his forebears. He has reforged a link in his memory which was broken when men abandoned the life of the nomad and moved from the forests, plains, and mountains to the security of villages. Having bridged the gap, he swiftly discovers something he had lost, a sense of belonging to the earth and to his kind. When that happens, he reaches back beyond his own life experience to a time when existence was simple.

So deeply ingrained is his feeling, and all it connotes, that even the building of a fire has ritualistic significance. Whether he admits it or not, every act of preparation is vital and satisfying to civilized man. Although the fire may not be needed for warmth or protection or even the preparation of food, it is still a primal and psychological necessity. On any wilderness expedition it always serves as a climax to the adventures of the day, is as important to a complete experience as the final curtain to a play. It gives everyone an opportunity to participate in an act hallowed by the devotion of forgotten generations.

The choice of the proper spot to build a fire is important. No place is picked lightly, for there are many factors involved. From the time man first carried a living brand from some lightning-struck stub and then discovered how to generate a flame with a whirling spindle and tinder, he was set apart. He has not forgotten, and even today everyone is anxious to help the fire-builder get started. All join in the search for kindling, for resinous bits of wood and bark. How proudly each brings in his offering, what genuine satisfaction is shared when the flames take hold! As the fire burns, see how it is tended and groomed and fondled, how little chips are added as they fall away from the larger sticks, how every man polices the fringe before him and treats the blaze as the living thing it is.

Anyone who has traveled in the wilds knows how much he looks forward to the time of day when he can lay down his burden and make camp. He pictures the ideal place and all that he must find there: water, a good wood supply, protection from wind and weather. As shadows begin to lengthen, the matter of a campsite takes precedence over everything else, as it has for ages past whenever men have been on the move. The camp with its fire has always been the goal, a place worth striving toward and, once attained, worth defending against all comers.

G. M. Trevelyan once said: "We are literally children of the earth, and removed from her our spirits wither or run to various forms of insanity. Unless we can refresh ourselves at least by intermittent contact with nature, we grow awry." What he was thinking of was the need of a race of men in which ancient needs and urges are still very much alive, a race caught in the intricate and baffling milieu of a civilization that no longer provides the old satisfactions or sources of contentment.

Thoreau implied exactly the same when he said: "In wilderness is the salvation of mankind." The campfire would have typified a necessary means of contact to them both.

In years of roaming the wilds, my campfires seem like glowing beads in a long chain of experience. Some of the beads glow more than the others, and when I blow on them ever so softly, they burst into flame. When that happens, I recapture the scenes themselves, pick them out of the almost forgotten limbo of the past and make them live.

One of these glowing beads was a little camp on a bare shelf of rock beside the Isabella River. The moon was full that night and the tent was in the light of it. Because the river ran north and south at that point, the moon shone down the length of a long, silvery pool, turning the rapids at its base into a million dancing pinpoints. A whippoorwill was calling and the valley of the Isabella was full of its haunting music, a music that seemed to blend into the gurgle of the rapids, the splash of rising trout, and the sleepy calling of a white-throated sparrow disturbed by the crackling flames.

The tall spruces at the end of the pool were black against the sky, and every leaf was tinged with silver. A trout rose again and again, and widening circles moved over the pool, erasing the smooth luminescence of its surface. The campfire was part of the magic and witchery of that scene. For primitive man the night might have been tinged with superstition and perhaps with fear. We only wondered at its beauty.

One summer I made an expedition into the Maligne River country in the Quetico. We were camped on a slender spit of rock overlooking the wild, island-studded reaches of Lac la Croix. A dead pine had fallen and shattered itself on the very tip of the point, and there with chunks of the resinous wood we built our fire. We sat on a little shelf of rock under the pines where we could watch the firelight change the branches and their tracery to coppery gold. For hours we watched them and the reflection on the water, but when a loon called from the open lake and then swam like a ghost into the circle of light, the scene was touched with magic.

Another time, I was camped at the mouth of the Range River where it empties into Low Lake. The bluebills had come and gone, and a snowstorm was raging overhead. Our tent was in the shelter of a ledge that protected us from the gale. It smelled of balsam, and our sleeping-bags were dry and warm. The little campfire out in front not only meant warmth and protection from the cold, but somehow made us part of the storm. Through it we could watch the swirling snow, hear it hiss as it struck the water, see the branches of the trees and the ground becoming whiter and whiter. Once, above its whispering and the roar of the wind, we heard the sound of wings, a last belated flock hurtling down the river.

There have been countless campfires, each one different, but some so blended into their backgrounds that it is hard for them to emerge. But I have found that when I catch even a glimmer of their almost forgotten light in the eyes of some friend who has shared them with me, they begin to flame once more. Those old fires have strange and wonderful powers. Even their memories make life the adventure it was meant to be.

CHAPTER XV

PINE KNOTS

Pine knots are different from ordinary firewoods. They cannot be compared with birch or aspen or oak, for the time-and-effort cost of gathering them is beyond the realm of common sense and reason. The warmth they give is negligible, but the light effects when they burn have a quality and importance that none of the others can approach. The burning of an old pine knot is a spiritual occasion, and the possession of a goodly supply for winter nights before the fireplace is a joy.

It was late October when I made my last expedition for knots. I say "expedition" because each foray after the prized nuggets of resin is more like a hunting-trip than ordinary wood-gathering. You just do not go into the woods anywhere, but must know the terrain and something about the ecology of the forests in order to know where to find them. More important than anything else is to be in the proper frame of mind, to recognize their worth, and to embark in a spirit of adventure.

Ice was forming in the protected bays of the lake the day I set forth. There was barely a quarter of an inch near shore, but enough to scratch the sides of the canoe. The leaves were gone and only in the hollows was there any remnant of the rusty bronze of the birches. Even the old gold of the tamaracks had disappeared and now they stood sere and gray in the bogs, waiting for the snow. The grasses were yellowed and in a little bay were covered with frost crystals. As the canoe slipped by, they moved suddenly in a breath of air and the bay sparkled with millions of sequins. A lone flock of bluebills took wing from the open water, circled warily, and disappeared over the horizon.

I landed the canoe on a grassy slope crowned with birches. Here at one time grew tall pines—not that there were any stumps or logs in evidence, but the mounds that marked their falling showed me where they had lain. Underneath the leaves and the duff were the knots, hard and sound and heavy. They would burn like torches, hold their flames as though unwilling to squander the energy they had held so long.

Near the landing I found several weathered to a silver gray, pointed spindles washed and polished by the waves until they were smooth and symmetrical. They had come from a pine that had dropped toward the water, and I could see its ancient top in the depths away from shore.

When I explored beneath the leaves, I found some sections of wood with the knots still in place. A blow of the ax and they were free for the taking. But mostly the knots lay by themselves with the brown disintegration of bark and wood still around them. I soon had a good pile of them down by the canoe.

Here was the same primitive satisfaction one finds fishing and hunting or in picking berries. The closest thing to it in wood-gathering is the stealing from abandoned beaver lodges of peeled and clean sticks of aspen that have served their purpose long ago. Like finding knots, it is living off the country, bringing in something from the wilds which no one else could find for you, something you would not want anyone else to do because of the joy of doing it yourself.

Knowing how the knots were made gives them significance, makes them unique and different from any other plant structure. All pines have resin ducts through which the golden fluid travels from the roots to the highest twigs. Where branches leave the main trunk, these ducts are bent, and because of the bending the flow of resin is dammed, saturating and completely impregnating the wood fibers. The same thing happens in gnarled and twisted roots, in any place where the free flow of resin is slowed. Although a great log may crumble into dust, the resin-soaked knots are impervious to decay and stay on for many years.

That night I stopped at the cabin of an old woodsman who felt about knots and resinous wood as I did. We had in common a vast respect for pine and what it could do. Before I crawled into my sleeping-bag, I watched him go through the ritual he had followed for many years. In back of his barrel stove were several sticks of red pine, sticks as dry and full of pitch as he could find. I watched him select a piece, turn it over carefully in his hands, then seat himself with his back against the wall.

Very deliberately he shaved off the first long shavings, each one curling beautifully as it left the blade. The longer and thinner the shaving, the better the curl; the tighter the curl, the quicker the flame. The knife sliced through again and again, and with each slice the contentment on the face of my friend seemed to grow. He contemplated the pile with satisfaction and watched the shavings twist and curl as though they were alive in the warmth of the barrel stove.

"Nothing better," he said. "Got a fine smell, too." He handed me a stick to smell. "That would explode when the flame hit it," he said.

The pile of feathered sticks and shavings was large enough. He pushed it carefully away from the stove to a spot against the wall where it would bask in the heat most of the night and in the morning be crisp and ready to flame. He sheathed his knife, for the ritual was over, the same ritual that in thousands of cabins and farm kitchens all over the land had been routine for generations. Here was real work, as important in its way as the setting of bread or the breaking of ground. This was purposeful, primitive, and satisfying, and most surely promoted pleasant dreams.

How much better, I thought, would it be for city nerves if at the close of each day a man could put his back to the wall and in the warmth of a barrel stove, with the wind and sleet whipping into a gale outside, whittle himself a pile of fragrant pine shavings. How much more serene his slumbers than if he simply checked his thermostat.

When I returned home the following day, I stored my knots in a special place where no one would make the mistake of taking them for ordinary wood. After hunting for them, packing them across the portages, and paddling them down several waterways, I would not let them be burned indiscriminately. They were reserved for special occasions when there was good talk, and music, and when the fire had burned to a deep bed of coals. Then, with the stage set for reverie, was the time to go down to the cache.

On one such night I picked a knot I knew well. A large one, it had come from a big lower branch of a pine that had grown by itself close to the shore of the little rock-bound lake where I had found the rest. That pine was a sapling when the first voyageurs came through on their trading-expeditions some three hundred years ago, was well grown at the time of the

American Revolution, crashed to earth during some storm before the loggers moved in sixty years ago. There it lay while the younger pines around it were harvested, and disintegrated slowly as the birch came in. Its knots survived a great fire that swept the area as an aftermath of the logging, lying there hidden beneath the duff and away from the heat.

I tucked the knot in among the glowing coals, where it was quietly caressed by exploring tongues of flame. It began to burn, gently at first, the yellows, blues, and reds of the resins bathing its black surface with strange lights. Here was the accumulated sunlight of bygone days giving off its warmth once more, the sun that had shone over the Quetico-Superior centuries before we were born. Now it was ours to share, and with it, all that the pine had known throughout its life. That pine knot was a concentration not only of energy but of the country itself. Burning it was the climax not only to its growth but to the expedition on which I found it.

CHAPTER XVI

NORTHERN LIGHTS

THE lights of the aurora moved and shifted over the horizon. Sometimes there were shafts of yellow tinged with green, then masses of evanescence which moved from east to west and back again. Great streamers of bluish white zigzagged like a tremendous trembling curtain from one end of the sky to the other. Streaks of yellow and orange and red shimmered along the flowing borders. Never for a moment were they still, fading until they were almost completely gone, only to dance forth again in renewed splendor with infinite combinations and startling patterns of design.

The lake lay like a silver mirror before me, and from its frozen surface came subterranean rumblings, pressure groans, sharp reports from the newly forming ice. As far as I could see, the surface was clear and shining. That ice was something to remember here in the north, for most years the snows come quickly and cover the first smooth glaze of freezing almost as soon as it is formed, or else the winds ruffle the surface of the crystallizing water and fill it with ridges and unevenness. But this time there had been no wind or snow to interfere, and the ice everywhere was clear—seven miles of perfect skating, something to dream about in years to come.

Hurriedly I strapped on my skates, tightened the laces, and in a moment was soaring down the path of shifting light which stretched endlessly before me. Out in the open away from shore there were few cracks—stroke—stroke—stroke—long and free, and I knew the joy that skating and skiing can give, freedom of movement beyond myself. But to get the feel of soaring, there must be miles of distance and conditions must be right. As I sped down the lake, I was conscious of no effort, only of the dancing lights in the sky and a sense of lightness and exaltation.

Shafts of light shot up into the heavens above me and concentrated there in a final climactic effort in which the shifting colors seemed drained from the horizons to form one gigantic rosette of flame and yellow and greenish purple. Suddenly I grew conscious of the reflections from the ice itself and that I was skating through a sea of changing color caught between the streamers above and below. At that moment I was part of the aurora, part of its light and of the great curtain that trembled above me.

Those moments of experience are rare. Sometimes I have known them while swimming in the moonlight, again while paddling a canoe when there was no wind and the islands seemed inverted and floating on the surface. I caught it once when the surf was rolling on an ocean coast and I was carried on the crest of a wave that had begun a thousand miles away. Here it was once more—freedom of movement and detachment from the earth.

Down the lake I went straight into the glistening path, speeding through a maze of changing color—stroke—stroke—stroke—the ringing of steel on ice, the sharp, reverberating rumbles of expansion below. Clear ice for the first time in years, and the aurora blazing away above it.

At the end of the lake I turned and saw the glittering lights of Winton far behind me. I lay down on the ice to rest. The sky was still bright and I watched the shifting lights come and go. I knew what the astronomers and the physicists said, that they were caused by sunspots and areas of gaseous disturbance on the face of the sun that bombarded the earth's stratosphere with hydrogen protons and electrons which in turn exploded atoms of oxygen, nitrogen, helium, and the other elements surrounding us. Here were produced in infinite combinations all the colors of the spectrum. It was all very plausible and scientific, but tonight that explanation left me cold. I was in no mood for practicality, for I had just come skating down the skyways themselves and had seen the aurora from the inside. What did the scientists know about what I had done? How could they explain what had happened to me and the strange sensations I had known?

Much better the poem of Robert Service telling of the great beds of radium emanating shafts of light into the northern darkness of the Yukon and how men went mad trying to find them. How infinitely more satisfying to understand and feel the great painting by Franz Johnson of a lone figure crossing a muskeg at night with the northern lights blazing above it. I stood before that painting in the Toronto Art Gallery one day and caught all the stark loneliness, all the beauty and the cold of that scene, and for a moment forgot the busy city outside.

I like to think of them as the ghost dance of the Chippewas. An Indian once told me that when a warrior died, he gathered with his fellows along the northern horizon and danced the war dances they had known on earth. The shifting streamers and the edgings of color came from the giant headdresses they wore. I was very young when I first saw them that way, and there were times during those enchanted years when I thought I could distinguish the movements of individual bodies as they rushed from one part of the sky to another. I knew nothing then of protons or atoms and saw the northern lights as they should be seen. I knew, too, the wonderment that only a child can know and a beauty that is enhanced by mystery.

As I lay there on the ice and thought of these things I wondered if legendry could survive scientific truth, if the dance of the protons would replace the ghost dance of the Chippewas. I wondered as I began to skate toward home if anything—even knowing the physical truth—could ever change the beauty of what I had seen, the sense of unreality. Indian warriors, exploding atoms, beds of radium—what difference did it make? What counted was the sense of the north they gave me, the fact that they typified the loneliness, the stark beauty of frozen muskegs, lakes, and forests. Those northern lights were part of me and I of them.

On the way back I noticed that there was a half-moon over the cluster of lights in the west. I skirted the power dam at the mouth of the Kawishiwi River, avoiding the blaze of its light on the black water below the spillway. Then suddenly the aurora was gone and the moon as well.

Stroke—stroke—stroke—the shores were black now, pinnacled spruce and shadowed birch against the sky. At the landing I looked back. The ice was still grumbling and groaning, still shaping up to the mold of its winter bed.

CHAPTER XVII

TIMBER WOLVES

I could hear them plainly now on both sides of the river, could hear the brush crack as they hurdled windfalls in their path. Once I thought I saw one, a drifting gray shadow against the snow, but it was only a branch swaying in the light of the moon. When I heard the full-throated bawling howl, I should have had chills racing up and down my spine. Instead, I was thrilled to know that the big grays might have picked up my trail and were following me down the glistening frozen highway of the river.

It was a beautiful night for travel—twenty below, and the only sound the steady swish and creak of my snowshoes on the crust. There was a great satisfaction in knowing that the wolves were in the country, that it was wild enough and still big enough for them to roam and hunt. That night the wilderness of the Quetico-Superior was what the voyageurs had known two hundred years before, as primitive and unchanged as before discovery.

Some months before, I had had the same kind of experience on a pack trip in the Sun River country of Montana. In the bottom of a canyon I saw the fresh track of a big grizzly in the soft muck beside a glacial creek. Although I did not see the bear, I knew it was near by. Those tracks changed the country immediately for me. From that moment on, it was the land of Lewis and Clark, the land of the mountain men of the last century, a valley of the old west.

The river ahead narrowed down to where two points of timber came out from either bank, and as I approached, I sensed instinctively the possibilities of attack. I was familiar with the wolf lore of the Old World, the packs on the steppes of Russia, the invasion of farms and villages, and had I believed the lurid tales of our early settlers and explorers, I might have been afraid. To the best of my knowledge, however, including the files of the U.S. Fish and Wildlife Service, for the past twenty-five years there has never been a single authenticated instance of unprovoked attack on man.

But still there was a feeling of uneasiness and apprehension, and I knew that if the animals were concerned with anything but satisfying their curiosity, the narrows would be the place for a kill. A swift rush from both points at the same time, a short, unequal scuffle in the snow, and it would be all over. My bones would go down with the ice in the spring, and no one would ever hear the story and no one would be able to explain.

As I neared the points of spruce, I could almost hear the crash of heavy bodies against windfalls and brush. Weighing a hundred, even as much as a hundred and twelve pounds or more, timber wolves are huge and powerful, can bring down a caribou or a moose, have nothing to fear on the entire continent but man. This was not the first time I had felt they were playing their game of hide-and-seek with me. On other lone midwinter expeditions I had sensed that they were close—a hunch perhaps, but as instinctive a reaction when in their immediate range as though I had actually seen them. I knew, as I hiked along that night, that I was being watched, a lone dark spot moving slowly along the frozen river.

That very morning I had seen where they had pulled down an old buck on the ice of a little lake, seen how they had run the deer to exhaustion and then sliced at his hamstrings, his flanks, and his throat, seen the long crimson spurt where they had ripped the jugular, seen the bits of mangled hide on the snow. He had been large and his horns were broad and palmate, but in the trampled bloody circle where he had made his last stand, he had not lasted long. He might have died slowly of starvation or disease, but he died as he should when his time had come, fighting for his life against his age-old ene- mies, dying like the valiant warrior he was out on the open ice.

The wolves had not eaten much, only the entrails and the viscera, but they would return, I knew, to satisfy themselves again. Such was the habit of their kind until we interfered with poison and trap and taught them caution and fear. When that happened, they learned to leave the carcasses after the first feeding and killed more than they would have normally. That kill was part of the age-old cycle of dependency be- tween the wolves and the deer. The predators, by the elim- ination of the old, the weak, and the diseased, improved the character of the herd and kept the younger and more virile breeding-stock alert and aware of danger. The deer provided food when there was no other source, when the heavy snows hid small rodents, the fish and snakes, grubs and berries and birds that gave the wolves sustenance during all other seasons of the year. There on the ice was evidence of the completed cycle, and, though all kills are gruesome things, I was glad to see it, for it meant a wilderness in balance, a primitive country that as yet had not been tamed.

In the narrows the spruces stood tall and black against the sky. The shores there were only a stone's throw apart. I must walk straight down the center, must not run, must not break my pace; and suddenly I was aware that, in spite of reason and my knowledge of the predators, ancient reactions were coming to the fore, intuitive warnings out of the past. In spite of what I knew, I was responding to the imagined threat of the narrows like a stone-age hunter cut off from his cave.

Then, far ahead, way beyond the dangerous points, two shadows broke from cover and headed directly down the river toward me. I stopped, slipped off my pack, and waited. Nearer and nearer they came, running with the easy, loose-jointed grace that only the big timber wolves seem to have. A hundred yards away they stopped and tried to get my wind; they wove back and forth, swaying as they ran. Then, about fifty feet away they stopped and looked me over. In the moonlight their gray hides glistened and I could see the greenish glint of their eyes. Not a movement or a sound. We stood watching each other as though such meetings were expected and commonplace.

As suddenly as they had appeared, they whirled and were off down the river, two drifting forms against the ice. Never before had I been that close, possibly never again would I see the glint in timber wolves' eyes or have such a chance to study their free and fluid movement. Once more came the long howl, this time far back from the river, and then I heard them no more.

A little later I pushed open the door of the little cabin and touched a match to the waiting tinder in the stove. As I sat there listening to the roar of it and stowing away my gear, I realized fully what I had seen and what I had felt. Had it not been twenty below, I would have left the door opened wide so as not to lose the spell of the moonlit river and the pack ranging its shores.

After I was warmed through and had eaten my supper, I

stepped outside once more. The river was still aglisten, and the far shore looked black and somber. An owl hooted back in the spruce, and I knew what that meant in the moonlit glades. A tree cracked sharply with the frost, and then it was still, so still that I could hear the beating of my heart. At last I caught what I was listening for—the long-drawn quavering howl from over the hills, a sound as wild and indigenous to the north as the muskegs or the northern lights. That was wilderness music, something as free and untamed as there is on this earth.

Although thrilled to hear them once again, I was saddened when I thought of the constant war of extermination which goes on all over the continent. Practically gone from the United States, wolves are now common only in the Quetico-Superior country, in Canada, and in Alaska, and I knew the day might come when, because of man's ignorance, the great grays would be gone even from there. Just before leaving on my trip up the river I had seen a news story about the killing of six timber wolves by airplane hunters in the Rainy Lake country. The picture showed them strung up on the wing of the plane and the hunters proudly posed beside them. As I studied that picture and the applauding captions, I wondered if the day would ever come when we would understand the importance of wolves.

Knowing the nature of our traditions of the old frontier and the pioneer complex that still guides our attitudes toward wildlife, I realized that it might never come. We still do not realize that today we can enjoy the wilderness without fear,

still do not appreciate the part that predators play in the balanced ecology of any natural community. We seem to prefer
herds of semi-domesticated deer and elk and moose, swarms of
small game with their natural alertness gone. It is as though
we were interested in conserving only a meat supply and nothing of the semblance of the wild.

It was cold, bitterly cold, and I hurried back into the cabin
and crawled into my sleeping-bag in the corner bunk. Beside
me was my pack and in a pocket my brush-worn copy of
Thoreau. I took it out, thumbed through it by the light of the
candle.

"We need," he said, "to witness our own limits transgressed
and some life pasturing freely where we never wander."

CHAPTER XVIII

FLYING IN

Once long ago I decided to fly in to a wilderness lake that for years I had reached only after many days of paddling and portaging. I wanted to see if I could recapture the old feeling of solitude and remoteness I had always known there without paying for it as I had done in the past. I wanted to know if I could get the feel of wilderness as I always used to when camped in that faraway and lovely place. It was one of my first flights and a thrilling one for me. Roaring along in a bush pilot's plane not more than a thousand feet above the trees, I felt that until then I had traveled like a mole, burrowing through the timber and brush of portages, creeping slowly down the rivers and over the wind-roughened lakes.

Now for the first time I saw the country as a whole, the hundreds of wilderness lakes I had explored. From that height I saw it as a hawk might see it: the blue and green lacework of sprawling lakes and their connecting rivers, the level lawns of muskeg, the tufted roughness of spruce and pine on the uplands. This was different from the close, intimate years when I had known the intricate maze of canoe trails as a mole might know the turnings of its runways in the turf.

To the east lay Gabemichigami, my destination; to the south the white and brawling Kawishiwi; to the north the dark virgin timber of the Quetico; behind me—thirty hurtling, noise-packed minutes away—the pavements of the town I had left. The entire country seemed in flood, the network of waterways running into one another, filling all the valleys with their blue and white, every sunken spot between the hills.

I glanced at the map and saw that just ahead was Gabe-michigami, a tremendous gash between two steep ridges. The plane banked, circled, and then, like the hawk it was, dropped to its kill, spiraling downward until it swooped close over the reaching tops of the pines. It side-slipped between the tower-ing shores, and in a moment the pontoons were slapping the water as the plane nosed gently toward the shore.

The pilot threw out my pack, and I scrambled along the pontoon and jumped for the rocks. A farewell push and the wings turned toward the open lake once more. The engine roared and the plane moved out in a cloud of spray. A moment later it was in the air over the ridges, heading back toward town. I glanced at my watch. It was exactly thirty minutes since we took off and here I was alone, as I had planned it, deep in the heart of the wilderness at a point that normally would have taken several days of hard travel by canoe.

After the quiet had come again, I looked around me and found my old campsite as I had left it a year before. The balsam boughs were dried and withered over my bed and the pothooks were still in place over the fire. There was the same little creek tumbling down from the rocks in its escape from Little Saganaga to the east, the same swirling pool with its trout. I had dreamed of this spot, of being alone here for just one day, of taking one of the beautiful trout below the riffle and enjoying the old wilderness I had known. To my amazement, the dream had come true.

At first I could not realize the change, so violent had it been. Formerly, by the time I had reached this spot on the map, the country had had a chance to soak in and become a part of me. But as I stood listening to the far drone of the plane, I knew that I was still part of the environment I had left and that it would take time for the old feeling of wilderness to come.

I have known that feeling many times since. To leave New York in the evening and be in Los Angeles in the morning, or

Miami or Havana or Chicago in just a few hours, is a psychological shock. One is never prepared for the change of scene, and I sometimes wonder if one ever will be.

I strolled back over the portage to the dead water above the rapids and sat there a long time trying to recapture the feeling of accomplishment I had known the last time I came in, but all that came to me was the violent throbbing reaction to my flight and a jumble made up of the many things I had done in the last hour of preparation. When the tent was up and fresh boughs were cut for my bed, I busied myself with my rod and began to cast for a trout. Before long I had a fine three-pounder, one of the golden-brown lake trout that grow to their best in Gabemichigami. I caught three, all told, and for an hour had the excitement of good fishing.

But that night in front of the fire, listening to the loons and their echoing calls from Little Saganaga, Kekekabic, Ogish-gemuncie, and a hundred other lakes around, I knew the answer. This was what I had dreamed of doing, but for the first time in my life I had failed to work for the joy of knowing the wilderness; had not given it a chance to become a part of me. The last time it had taken three days of travel, many portages, sixty miles or more of bending to the paddle and fighting the wind, two campsites along the way, with always the great goal ahead, one of the most beautiful spots in the border country.

That vision alone had been enough to make my packs light and to take the sting from tired muscles. The thought of that camp with the creek singing away beside it was compensation enough. When at last after those days of travel my tent was actually pitched there, I knew real joy and happiness. This time it seemed that I had not earned the right to enjoy it.

The next afternoon the plane roared again over the horizon and in half an hour I was back to the automobiles, the pavements, and my friends. Yes, I had been on a flight, had gone far into the lake country, had taken a few trout and enjoyed myself, but inside I was still a little out of breath and somewhat baffled by what I had done. Seeing the country from the air had given me a bird's-eye view and perspective that I could not have in any other way, and the beauty was not lost to me.

I knew, however, what I must do the next time. I must go in with pack and canoe and work for the peace of mind which I knew could be found there. I would be a mole again and learn the feel of rocks under my feet, breathe the scent of balsam and spruce under the sun, feel the wetness of spray and muskeg, be part of the wilderness itself.

CHAPTER XIX

THE WAY OF A CANOE

THE movement of a canoe is like a reed in the wind. Silence is part of it, and the sounds of lapping water, bird songs, and wind in the trees. It is part of the medium through which it floats, the sky, the water, the shores.

A man is part of his canoe and therefore part of all it knows.

The instant he dips a paddle, he flows as it flows, the canoe yielding to his slightest touch, responsive to his every whim and thought. The paddle is an extension of his arm, as his arm is part of his body. Skiing down a good slope with the snow just right comes close to it, with the lightness of near-flight, the translating of even a whisper of a wish into swift action; there, too, is a sense of harmony and oneness with the earth. But to the canoeman there is nothing that compares with the joy he knows when a paddle is in his hand.

A rowboat has the fulcrum of the oarlock to control it and the energy of a man rowing is a secondary force, but in paddling the motion is direct; the fulcrum is the lower hand and wrist, and the force is transmitted without change or direction. Because of this there is correlation and control.

There is balance in the handling of a canoe, the feeling of its being a part of the bodily swing. No matter how big the waves or how the currents swirl, you are riding them as you would ride a horse, at one with its every motion. When the point is reached where the rhythm of each stroke is as poised as the movement of the canoe itself, weariness is forgotten and there is time to watch the sky and the shores without thought of distance or effort. At such a time the canoe glides along obedient to the slightest wish and paddling becomes as unconscious and automatic an effort as breathing. Should you be lucky enough to be moving across a calm surface with mirrored clouds, you may have the sensation of suspension between heaven and earth, of paddling not on the water but through the skies themselves.

If the waves are rolling and you are forced to make your way against them, there is the joy of battle, each comber an enemy to be thwarted, a problem in approach and defense. A day in the teeth of a gale—dodging from island to island, fighting one's way along the lee shore of some wind-swept point, only to dash out again into the churning water and the full force of the wind, then to do it again and again—is assurance that your sleep will be deep and your dreams profound.

There is a satisfaction in reaching some point on the map in spite of wind and weather, in keeping a rendezvous with some campsite that in the morning seemed impossible of achievement. In a canoe the battle is yours and yours alone. It is your muscle and sinew, your wit and courage against the primitive forces of the storm. That is why when after a day of battle your tent is pitched at last in the lee of some sheltering cliff, the canoe up safe and dry, and supper under way, there is an exaltation that only canoemen know.

Almost as great a challenge is running with the waves down some lake where the wind has a long unbroken sweep. Riding the rollers takes more than skill with a paddle; it takes an almost intuitive sense of the weight and size of them and a knowledge of how they will break behind you. A bad move may mean that a comber will wash the gunwales. A man must know not only his canoe and what it will do, but the meaning of the waves building up behind him. This is attack from the rear without a chance of looking back, a guessing at a power and lifting force that he cannot see. But what a fierce joy to be riding with a thousand white-maned horses racing with the wind down some wild waterway toward the blue horizons!

Rapids, too, are a challenge. Dangerous though they may be, treacherous and always unpredictable, no one who has known the canoe trails of the north does not love their thunder and the rush of them. No man who has portaged around white water, studied the swirls, the smooth, slick sweeps and the V's that point the way above the breaks, has not wondered if he should try. Rapids can be run in larger craft, in scows and rubber boats and rafts, but it is in a canoe that one really feels the river and the power of it.

Is there any suspense that quite compares with that moment of commitment when the canoe heads toward the lip of a long, roaring rapids and then is taken by its unseen power? At first there is no sense of speed, but suddenly you are part of it, involved in spume and spouting rocks. Then when there is no longer any choice and a man knows that his fate is out of hand, his is a sense of fierce abandonment when all the voyageurs of the past join the rapids in their shouting.

While the canoe is in the grip of the river, a man knows what detachment means, knows that, having entered the maelstrom, he is at its mercy until it has spent its strength. When through skill or luck he has gone through the snags, the reaching rocks, and the lunging billows, he needs no other accolade but the joy that he has known.

Only fools run rapids, say the Indians, but I know this: as long as there are young men with the light of adventure in their eyes and a touch of wildness in their souls, rapids will be run. And when I hear tales of smashed canoes and lives as well, though I join in the chorus of condemnation of the fools who take such chances, deep in my heart I understand and bid them *bon voyage*. I have seen what happens when food and equipment are lost far from civilization and I know what it takes to traverse a wilderness where they are no trails but the waterways themselves. The elements of chance and danger are wonderful and frightening to experience and, though I bemoan the recklessness of youth, I wonder what the world would be like without it. I know it is wrong, but I am for the spirit that makes young men do the things they do. I am for the glory that they know.

But more than shooting white water, fighting the gales, or running before them is the knowledge that no part of any country is inaccessible where there are waterways with portages between them. The canoe gives a sense of unbounded range and freedom, unlimited movement and exploration such as larger craft never know. Sailboats, rowboats, launches, and cruisers are hobbled by their weight and size to the waters on which they are placed. Not so a canoe. It is as free as the wind itself, can go wherever fancy dictates. The canoeman can camp each night in a different place, explore out-of-the-way streams and their sources, find hidden corners where no one has ever been.

Wherever there are waterways, there are connecting trails between them, portages used by primitive man for countless

centuries before discovery. Although overgrown and sometimes hard to find, they are always there, and when you pack
your outfit across them you are part of a great company that
has passed before. When you camp on ancient campsites,
those voyageurs of the past camp with you.

The feeling of being part of that tradition is one of the
reasons canoemen love the sound of a paddle and the feel of it
as it moves through the water. Long before the days of
mechanized transportation, long before men learned to use the
wheel, the waterways of the earth knew the dugout, the skin
hunting-boat, the canoe. A man feels at home with a paddle in
his hand, as natural and indigenous as with a bow or spear.
When he swings through a stroke and the canoe moves forward, he sets in motion long-forgotten reflexes, stirs up ancient
sensations deep within his subconscious.

When he has traveled for many days and is far from the
settlements of his kind, when he looks over his cruising-outfit
and knows it is all he owns, that he can travel with it to new
country as he wills, he feels at last that he is down to the real
business of living, that he has shed much that was unimportant
and is in an old, polished groove of experience. Life for some
strange reason has suddenly become simple and complete; his
wants are few, confusion and uncertainty gone, his happiness
and contentment deep.

There is magic in the feel of a paddle and the movement of
a canoe, a magic compounded of distance, adventure, solitude,
and peace. The way of a canoe is the way of the wilderness

and of a freedom almost forgotten. It is an antidote to in-security, the open door to waterways of ages past and a way of life with profound and abiding satisfactions. When a man is part of his canoe, he is part of all that canoes have ever known.

FROM

WILDERNESS DAYS

CHAPTER XX

THE FEEL OF SPRING

Spring canoe trips into the hinterlands are always exciting adventures after a northern winter, for impressions then seem as fresh as the country itself. One that stands out boldly from the many I have made over the years is a trip young Sig and I took during the war, when he was at home on a last furlough before going overseas with the 10th Mountain Division. I wanted him to carry something special away with him, something he would remember when the going got tough: the feel of spring and the joy of wilderness travel after the break-up.

It was in May, after the ice went out. The sun was shining as though to make up for lost time and the air was full of the smells of thawing earth, open water, and swelling buds. The shores of southern slopes were Nile green where the aspen stood. Ice crystals sparkled on sedges nearby, and in sheltered bays snowbanks still gleamed. The tinkle of melting ice was everywhere. Ducks whispered overhead and seagulls wheeled in arcs of silver in the morning light.

"Mountain air," said Sig. "This is the way it feels above timber line."

We stepped into the canoe and pushed off, happy to be paddling again, going into some back country forgotten by everyone except the loons and explorers such as we. Little lakes, creeks, and beaver flowages off the beaten routes beckoned irresistibly. Seldom seen or used, they were new as the spring was new. The canoe was pointed to the northeast, a chain of boggy waterways south of Knife on the Minnesota–Ontario border. My old friend Jean had told me about them when he heard Sig was coming home, and urged me to take him there to try for trout in one of the clear-water lakes.

"No big ones," he had said, "but they're mighty pretty, sort of a gold, speckled brown with reddish tips to their fins, and rose underneath."

Jean was an outlaw according to the wardens, and one of the finest woodsmen in the north, and what he knew about the maze of waterways in his domain was nobody's business but his own. Like all frontiersmen, he felt the country belonged to him, was his to use, that trapping was a game and regulations were for outsiders.

"No hard feelings," he told me once. "Those game wardens

have to make a living too, and it's their job to keep us out of the beaver country."

The country Jean traveled had always appealed to us, no matter how hard to reach, and going in was a challenge we accepted with delight. Portages were usually overgrown and hard to find, for they did not warrant the time and cost for rangers to keep them open. Beaver sloughs, tiny creeks crisscrossed with windfalls and with barely enough water to float a canoe, strings of little ponds between them—this was the kind of terrain he used.

As we paddled up Moose Lake, it seemed as though we were seeing it for the first time. Spring trips are always that way, and the old familiar route we were following to the beaver country was almost strange. Spring, in addition to many other things, is a time for renewal of memories that may have grown dim during the winter, so when we reached a point on Newfound Lake where Camp 25 used to be, I lingered.

It didn't mean much to Sig, but it did to me. The cabin was gone now. Once it had served as a stopping place for rangers, trappers, and lone travelers. Now it was down, except for a few foundation logs covered with long, brown grass and brambles. A bear had torn one of the logs apart for grubs, and a deer had pawed the earth to get at the salt where the stove had been. I wandered around, remembering bitter winter nights with the stars blazing and the mercury below zero, snowshoe trails leading in, long icicles from the eaves, wolves and foxes hanging from a pole—the winter I made the rounds of the poison trail.*

I could see again the yellow light of the window from the last bend in the trail, sniff the wood smoke and then, when the door opened wide, the warm smell of cooking, balsam boughs, the drying outfit. How bright that lantern used to be, how warm and friendly the cabin after a day in the bush. Everything was gone now with Bill and Jack and Gay and the rest—just a grass-grown mound of crumbling logs.

Sig brought me to with a start. "Let's go, Dad," he said. "We've quite a stretch to make before dark."

We left Camp 25 and passed into a narrows where deer crossed the ice during the winter and often broke through. Once, seven carcasses lay there frozen in the ice, food for wolves, foxes, and ravens. Somehow they never learned, kept coming winter after winter, though the dead lay plainly in sight. Their trail was an old one, and near the water's edge was bare gravel. We went in close, looked down to the bottom, and there in the mud were greenish-white bones.

Just beyond, we surprised a beaver sunning itself on a rock. It blinked lazily, watched us wide-eyed, slid off and slapped its tail. The channel led into a bay and at its end we could hear the Ensign River Rapids. We headed for the sound, fought the current, and landed on a grassy bank— the beginning of our first portage. It felt good to stretch our legs and feel the rocks under our feet. The river was high and

---

* Predator control in the old days by state and federal governments. Poison was used.

boiling. Fish were coming up to spawn—suckers, northern pike, walleyes—their black shadows holding steady in the flow.

Ensign was calm, its shores as misty green as those on Moose. A partridge drummed, a muffled hidden beat, steady and slow at first, then a swift crescendo, and when it was over the sunshine and quiet were even more intense than before. Halfway down the lake we stopped on a flat, rocky spit to boil a pot of tea.

"Portage out of the northeast end," said Sig, studying the map. "Two or three potholes and flowages and we're on our own."

We spent an hour soaking up the feel of the country, basking in the sun. The whiskyjacks found us swiftly and we fed them bits of bread and meat. A squirrel came down a jackpine and scolded us roundly. Ravens soared, watching the ground below. They knew the best places, the narrows where the deer broke through, the currents between the islands. Nothing ever escaped them. Ours was a sense of golden leisure that comes only in the spring, after months of grayness and cold.

At the end of the lake was a slow, flowing creek separated from the open water by a sandbar. It moved through a swamp grown thickly with sedges, cattails, and alder. A flock of mallards took off from the rushes and the sun glinted on green and bronze as they climbed.

Below the last riffle, we landed and looked for fish but saw none. The portage was low and soggy, and lush buds of marsh marigold showed greenish yellow against the mud. Finding no evidence of a trail, we threw on the packs and canoe and simply followed the bank of the creek. Going up a birch-grown slope we jumped a doe and a fawn, and a little farther on found a beaver pond with a house in its center. We dropped the canoe, pushed into the flowage, and paddled between great silvery boles of tamarack and spruce. Redwings sat on every cattail and shrub, the males flaunting their crimson epaulets and pouring their hearts out in gay *conkarees*. It was as though all the blackbirds in the north had congregated there that day to make us glad—and never for a moment were they still. This was a sound that comes only in May, when their singing is a warbling symphony to spring.

After the flowage, we portaged through alders and a tangle of willow until we found another widening, where we poled the canoe with our paddles and pulled it forward by holding on to the brush. All the time we were heading east.

"This is Jean's country, all right," said Sig, "exactly the sort of a layout he'd like."

At the far end of the valley we heard running water and went over to investigate. This was different from what we had seen; it was clear, and foaming white where it dropped over a ledge. A school of suckers lay with noses into the flow. We watched as they threw themselves over the rocks onto the ledge, to rest for a moment on their sides, then with a convulsive effort reached the pool above.

Sig reached down from the bow, slipped his hand into the gills of one of them, held it up for me to see. The fish squirmed powerfully and it was all he could do to keep his grip. Black on top, white with a rosy tint underneath, had it not been for the mouth it might have been beautiful.

"How about supper?" he said. "This time of year they're good."

"I'm not proud," I answered, "but let's wait. We're not starving yet."

He lowered the sucker gently into the boiling current and released it. For a while it was quiet, gills opening and closing, then with a lunge it was back in deep water again.

As we lifted the canoe onto the bank, the brush crashed and we glimpsed a black shadow heading up the creek. Portaging, we found several half-eaten fish the bear had been gorging on, as all bears do along the spawning streams of the north. We did not see it again, but heard it beside the creek; it did not want to leave its feeding.

After several portages we finally came onto the shore of a narrow lake about a mile in length. The slopes were rocky and covered with jackpine and spruce, and a spit of a point lay invitingly to one side. A loon called in greeting and the water sparkled in the sun.

"This is it," said Sig. "Here's the lake Jean told you about."

We were alone, with all the time we needed to explore its reefs and shallows, to find where the trout had spawned the fall before. There was no sign of a camp, no tent poles, or a fireplace, or marks of any kind. The site was virgin and unused. I didn't expect to find Jean's set-up in the open for, like all outlaws, he stayed back in the bush, left no telltale trails or ax marks that might give him away. He moved through his domain like an Indian, traveled only at night.

"Come here," said Sig excitedly. "I've found something."

I went over to him, and there beneath a gray, protruding ledge, hidden with moss and pine needles, he had found five rusty beaver traps.

"Here is the proof," he said. "This is his country."

He placed the traps back carefully under the ledge and covered them with moss.

The sun was down now, the lake beginning to glow. We built a fireplace out of the greenish-gray slabs of slate near the water's edge, pitched the tent as close to the fire as we dared, with a view down the lake. We could watch the fire before going to sleep, and would waken with a vista before us. Such things were important to us, though of course there was the hazard of a gale blowing sparks from the fire, or even of snow and rain, but those we were willing to face.

After supper the dusk settled quickly and the loons called as they always do south of Knife: long, rolling peals of laughter from every point of the compass, merging at last into a weird, continuous harmony that somehow epitomizes the spring break-up better than any other sound. There was magic in the air, and in the morning we would know if what Jean had said was true. It was good to lie there in our bags watching the glow of our dying fire and the deeper glow of sunset beyond; but most of all it was good to feel the ground again and to know we were back in a country we loved.

The day dawned clear, and as the sun burst over the ridges to the east we were bathed in its warmth. We cooked breakfast, assembled our gear, picked out flies and spinners on a chance the trout would be near shore. Anything could happen, there might be no reefs, the fish already deep. We followed the north side, casting the shallows all the way, but not a strike did we get.

"Might be too early," I said. "Sometimes they don't hit for several weeks after the ice goes out."

I wanted so desperately to get some trout for Sig's sake, but try as we might, nothing took hold. At the very end of the lake was a rocky peninsula, almost an island, with a shallow gravel reef between it and the shore. If ever there was a spot, this was it. If the trout had spawned there in the fall, they must still be close—but each time we drifted through it was the same.

We changed lures and went deeper, but all we caught were snags. By midafternoon a wind came up out of the east, clouds covered the sun, and it grew cold. We landed on the rock beside the reef and built a big fire out of windfalls. The gale increased and suddenly there was a drift of snow in the air. Once more we tried the shallows with the same result, then paddled back to camp without a word.

We tightened the tent ropes, cut a good supply of wood, got ready for the storm. The chickadees stopped their singing, squirrels and whiskyjacks disappeared, and by the time we crawled into our sleeping-bags the ground was white. For a long time we lay watching the flames, and went to sleep with the sound of snow and sleet hissing into the coals and whispering against the frozen tent.

Spring in the north is strange and wonderful and always full of change. We thought of the long paddle back, the slippery portages with an icy wind over the open reaches toward home.

"The sun will be out tomorrow," said Sig. "It's got to come out."

"It will," I replied, but I knew better with the blow coming out of the east.

Several inches of snow fell during the night and in the morning it looked like November. The water was leaden, the new green of the aspen-covered slopes now a bank of white. It was bitterly cold, the wind high, so we built up the fire, and I made a breakfast for explorers who needed strength and courage to face the day: porridge, bacon, eggs, bread, and plenty of hot coffee. As we basked in the warmth our spirits rose and we both had the same idea.

"Listen, Dad," said Sig, "there were a lot of dry logs on that rock. We could paddle over there, get a real blaze going, dash out to the narrows, fish for a while and come back to get warm."

"Besides," I told him excitedly, "this change of weather might just start the trout feeding. Sometimes this is all it takes."

We put on all the clothes we had, fought the waves to the ledge, and in a short time had a roaring fire under way. When we were thoroughly warmed again we pushed the canoe into the narrows and over the reef we had tried the day before.

Sig's first cast brought a strike and a good one, and I watched him land that fish as though I had never seen it done before. This would tell the story. The trout fought hard, raced under the canoe, went down and surfaced once. Tiring, it came close. I reached down and lifted it into the canoe. A beauty it was, golden brown with reddish fins, a decided blush of color along the sides. We hooted with joy and laughed as the snow swirled around us. By that time we were both so numb we were forced to return. Another log, and the blaze went high. We slapped our hands together, pummeled each other roundly, and soaked up the heat until we were ready once more.

This time it was my turn, and in a moment I had one as beautiful as the first—only a couple of pounds, but as hard, firm, and well colored as any trout I'd seen. Again we sped back to get warm.

The next time we both fished, hooked two trout at once and got our lines so hopelessly snarled it took an hour to get them untangled. By noon we had all the law allowed, paddled back to camp happy as two *voyageurs* could ever be. We had found our little lake and the trout Jean had told us about. What is more, we had caught them in a howling snowstorm on flies and spinners.

That night we celebrated and each of us had a fish for supper, knowing they would never taste so good again. Trout fried to a golden brown, hush puppies in the fat, a can of beans and tea. We piled logs on the fire and crawled contentedly into our bags. The storm could howl now and we didn't care. Tomorrow was another day.

In the morning we took down the frozen tent, packed the outfit, and started down the creek the way we had come, slipping and sliding over rocks and windfalls, snow whipping our faces from the brush. A smooth, rocky slope we had come over easily was treacherous now, and once I fell with the canoe. Another time we crossed a rocky stream bed, its boulders covered with a smooth, unbroken blanket of white. Each step was a gamble, a chance for a broken leg or a sprained ankle.

But paddling was the worst, with gusts of snow and spray freezing onto our clothes, until it was hard to bend our arms. Mitts were of no use and our frostbitten hands took a beating. At each portage we stopped to build a fire, and several times debated whether to go on or to pitch camp until the storm had blown itself out. Only one hitch to that: Sig was soon due at Camp Hale and the end of his furlough was near. So we abandoned any thought of giving in, fought our way down mile by frozen mile, past Camp 25, down Newfound and the full sweep of Moose.

By late afternoon we were at the landing at the south end of the lake where our cruise had begun four days before. We unloaded, went back to the water and stood looking down the lake. White-flecked combers and blowing drift were out there. Then the sun burst through a rift in the gray, scudding clouds and for a glorious instant the waters were blue again and the shores dazzling with silver and Nile green. We looked at each other and laughed. We had won, found what we had gone in for—the feel of spring—and had some trout as proof. We had known the thrill of exploring forgotten country together, and had seen it at its best.